THE
WINGED LIFE

THE POETIC VOICE OF
HENRY DAVID THOREAU

edited and with commentaries by ROBERT BLY

wood engravings by MICHAEL McCURDY

HarperPerennial

A Division of HarperCollins*Publishers*

THE WINGED LIFE. Preface, commentaries and biographical sketch copyright © 1986 by Robert Bly. Illustrations copyright © 1986 by Michael McCurdy. Poems by Thoreau are reprinted from *Collected Poems of Henry Thoreau*, copyright © 1970 by Carl Bode, by permission of The John Hopkins University Press. All rights reserved. Printed in the United States of America. No part of this book may be used or reproduced in any manner whatsoever without written permission except in the case of brief quotations embodied in critical articles and reviews. For information address HarperCollins Publishers, Inc., 10 East 53rd Street, New York, NY 10022.

HarperCollins books may be purchased for educational, business, or sales promotional use. For information, please call or write: Special Markets Department, HarperCollins Publishers, Inc., 10 East 53rd Street, New York, NY 10022. Telephone: (212) 207-7528; Fax: (212) 207-7222.

First HarperPerennial edition published 1992.

LIBRARY OF CONGRESS CATALOG CARD NUMBER 91-50512

ISBN 0-06-097453-2

THE WINGED LIFE

TABLE OF CONTENTS

This book gathers and presents my own view of Henry David Thoreau and cele-brates the 140th anniversary of his departure to Walden Pond. Thoreau wrote some marvelous poems, which deserve to be known. They are not many. Some of his greatest poetry lies secretively glowing in his prose, as Thoreau himself implied when he remarked that he had two notebooks, one for facts and one for poems, and he often had difficulty deciding where a certain passage belonged. Pound said poetry should be at least as well written as prose, and I have selected from Thoreau's journals, essays and travel books prose pieces that are at least as well written as poems, and have mingled the two forms here. I enjoy moving from his poetry to his prose and back; as often as I could, I've placed poetry and prose on the same subjects together, so that one can feel the contrast.

His poetry and his prose make a contrast. Thoreau's genius lay in what the German poet Novalis called a sober and spontaneous observation of the outer world, and the poetic tradition he inherited—from Milton, Pope and Wordsworth —provided no model for lines composed exclusively of observed detail. In Words-worth, superb detail is interrupted by stretches of emotional and philosophical discourse. The poem able to float a cargo of detail, launched in 1855 by Whitman and manned later by Gerard Manley Hopkins, William Carlos Williams, Marianne Moore, William Stafford, James Wright, Galway Kinnell and many others, had not entered the waters when Thoreau began to write. His inability to load the metrical poem with observed facts was probably one reason why, after writing many poems in his earlier years, he gradually abandoned poetry. The details he loved appeared in prose sentences composed with immense care for rhythm and vigor of expression.

This anthology, then, mingles prose passages and poetry. Those who want more poems without admixture should go to the *Collected Poems*, edited by Carl Bode. I have shaped the book by restricting it to five sections, each centering on a stage of Thoreau's thought-life. The first section, which I call The Bug in the Table, recognizes the secret life buried or hidden inside each of us. The second group of texts observes that human beings live meanly despite that secret presence. The third turns to Thoreau's own decision not to live meanly and his endurance of the consequent moratorium, or waiting period; and the fourth to the genius of his seeing, his devoted and precise observation of the nonhuman world. The last sec-tion concentrates on wildness, Thoreau's own and the wildness he loved in nature.

PART ONE

The Bug in the Table

THOREAU WAS SURE that we could have an original love affair with the universe, but only if we decline to marry the world, and he suspected that the divine man is the man uncontrolled by social obligation. He believed that the young man or young woman should give up tending the machine of civilization and instead farm the soul. We can sense the boundaries of our soul, whose stakes are set thousands of miles out in space, only if we disintegrate property boundaries here on earth. When we fight for the soul and its life, we receive as reward not fame, not wages, not friends, but what is already in the soul, a freshness that no one can destroy, that animals and trees share.

The most important word is *soul*. All of the ideas referred to above are really a single idea, one massive truth, and we can call that truth the Truth of Concord, the Green Mountain Truth, the truth believed in the Bronze Age, the truth of the soul's interior abundance.

To many Americans in the generation of the 1840s it felt as if the United States had fallen into mesmeric attention to external forces, and a shameless obedience to them. The swift development of the Northeast, with its numerous factories, its urban workshops for immigrants, its network of free-acting capitalists, its centralized industry, showed that external forces can and do overwhelm forces of soul and conscience, changing everyone's life for the worse. To many in New England it felt as if some sort of Village King had been killed; the ancient, grounded religious way was passing; a new dispensation had arrived. The sovereign of the new administration was not a king or a human being, but what Blake called "a ratio of numbers," and this ominous, bodiless king lived in the next county, the next state, the next planet. Living under the power of a bodiless king is a bad way to live.

A man who lived in the Concord area, fourteen years older than Thoreau and with a fierce, bold and reckless mind—I mean Ralph Waldo Emerson—introduced his statement of the truth of the soul's abundance in this way in his essay "Nature":

To go into solitude, a man needs to retire as much from his chamber as from society. I am not solitary whilst I read and write, though nobody is with me. But if a man would be alone, let him look at the stars. . . .

. . . In the presence of nature a wild delight runs through the man, in spite of real sorrows. . . . Crossing a bare common, in snow puddles, at twilight, under a clouded sky, without having in my thoughts any occurrence of special good fortune, I have enjoyed a perfect exhilaration. I am glad to the brink of fear. In the woods, too, a man casts off his years, as the snake his slough, and at what period soever of life is always a child. In the woods is perpetual youth.

The direction could not be clearer. We don't expect this man to urge the establishment of vocational schools, or to praise the trickle-down philosophy of heavy industry, or to believe that amassing wealth is evidence of divine favor. These words move toward the soul, not toward manipulation of matter, and when we have arrived within the soul the motion is not lateral, but downward and upward:

Standing on the bare ground,—my head bathed by the blithe air and uplifted into infinite space,— all mean egotism vanishes. I become a transparent eyeball. ("Nature")

The metaphor, though well known, remains astonishing: the transparent eyeball. The emphasis on transparency tells us that Emerson does not intend to occupy the castle of sorrow and the kingdom of melancholy, nor to descend into the dungeon of the body, but that he wants to recruit an army for a charge into the infinite, desperate as the Light Brigade's. He wants inside him an army disciplined, ascetic, single-minded; an army with few baggage trains, living in floorless tents on dried food. His quest will be to marry nature for vision, rather than for possession. His aim is not to live more but to see more.

Emerson, in "Nature," goes on: "I am nothing; I see all; the currents of the Universal Being circulate through me." As he says that, it is clear he is not talking of a narrow or tribal god, and he finishes the passage by saying, "I am part and parcel of God."

The truth that we have been circling around with images of journey, similes of battle, metaphors taken from the history of love, amounts, as suggested, to one essential truth. It is a lucky generation that hears it, because it is one of the few truths on which a young person can ground his or her life.

Many young men and women want to marry nature for vision, not possession. Some, having accomplished by their late twenties no deed worth praise, feel insignificant and scorned. The world scorns football players who make no yardage, writers who do not publish, fishermen who catch no fish. But the soul truth, which young people, when lucky, pick up from somewhere—perhaps in Emerson's phrasing, perhaps in someone else's—sustains them. If the world doesn't feed them, they receive some nourishment from this truth. The substance of the truth goes to their paws, and they live through the winter of scorn and despicability in the way hibernating bears were once thought to live, by sucking their own paws.

The soul truth assures the young man or woman that if not rich, he or she is still in touch with truth; that his inheritance comes not from his immediate parents but from his equals thousands of generations ago; that the door to the soul is unlocked; that he does not need to please the doorkeeper, but that the door in front of him is his, and intended for him, and the doorkeeper obeys when spoken to. It implies that nature is not below the divine, but is itself divine, "perpetual youth." Most important of all, the soul truth assures the young man or woman that despite the Industrial Revolution certain things are as they have always been, and that in human growth the road of development goes through nature, not around it.

I think one reason the Thoreau-Melville-Hawthorne generation wrote so much great literature is that this fundamental soul truth, well phrased by Emerson, Horace Bushnell and other writers, and untainted yet by mockery, came through freshly to mind and body. Forty years later Yeats was fed by this truth, phrased this time by Blake and Edwin Ellis, and supported by old Celtic stories. Yeats expressed the truth in a very different way, but if we listen we can hear it throughout his poem "Paudeen":

> Indignant at the fumbling wits, the obscure spite
> Of our old Paudeen in his shop, I stumbled blind
> Among the stones and thorn-trees, under morning light;
> Until a curlew cried and in the luminous wind
> A curlew answered; and suddenly thereupon I thought
> That on the lonely height where all are in God's eye,
> There cannot be, confusion of our sound forgot,
> A single soul that lacks a sweet crystalline cry.

Yeats, like Thoreau, recognized that marrying nature for vision, rather than for possession, creates a luminous place inside that every human being longs for. He calls it "the townland":

There's many a strong farmer
Whose heart would break in two,
If he could see the townland
That we are riding to;

The truth that nourished Thoreau in 1847 had nourished Goethe a half-century earlier, and he ended his great poem "The Holy Longing" with these two stanzas:

Distance does not make you falter
now, arriving in magic, flying—
and, finally, insane for the light,
you are the butterfly and you are gone.

And so long as you haven't experienced
this: to die and so to grow,
you are only a troubled guest
on the dark earth.

In this section there are nineteen texts—some poems, others passages from his journals or from *Walden*—in which Thoreau, using the bricks of his intricate and precise detail, builds a house for this truth. His walls are more solid than Emerson's. Thoreau wrote a few good metrical poems on the soul truth, but his prose on the subject is exquisite, high-spirited and elegant. The anecdote of the insect egg he tells very well. The egg remained for years inside the trunk of an apple tree, undisturbed even when the carpenter cut down the tree and made it into a table, and rested dormant there until, warmed one day, perhaps by a coffee pot set above it, it hatched out at last. This is a marvelous tale, and by the anecdote Thoreau suggests that inside us, too, there may be a winged life that is not visible to us when we sit at a table, or become a table. The story suggests that there is an unhatched abundance inside us that we ourselves have not prepared. Our psyche at birth was not a schoolchild's slate with nothing written on it, but rather an apple-wood table full of eggs. We receive at birth the residual remains of a billion lives before us.

Every one has heard the story which has gone the rounds of New England, of a strong and beautiful bug which came out of the day leaf of an old table of apple-tree wood, which had stood in a farmer's kitchen for sixty years, first in Connecticut, and afterward in Massachusetts,—from an egg deposited in the living tree many years earlier still, as appeared by counting the annual layers beyond it; which was heard gnawing out for several weeks, hatched perchance by the heat of an urn. Who does not feel his faith in a resurrection and immortality strengthened by hearing of this? Who knows what beautiful and winged life, whose egg has been buried for ages under many concentric layers of woodenness in the dead dry life of society, deposited at first in the alburnum of the green and living tree, which has been gradually converted into the semblance of its well-seasoned tomb,—heard perchance gnawing out now for years by the astonished family of man, as they sat round the festive board,—may unexpectedly come forth from amidst society's most trivial and handselled furniture, to enjoy its perfect summer life at last!

I do not say that John or Jonathan will realize all this; but such is the character of that morrow which mere lapse of time can never make to dawn. The light which puts out our eyes is darkness to us. Only that day dawns to which we are awake. There is more day to dawn. The sun is but a morning star.

Walden, "Conclusion"

The moon now rises to her absolute rule,
And the husbandman and hunter
Acknowledge her for their mistress.
Asters and golden reign in the fields
And the life everlasting withers not.
The fields are reaped and shorn of their pride
But an inward verdure still crowns them.
The thistle scatters its down on the pool
And yellow leaves clothe the river—
And nought disturbs the serious life of men.
But behind the sheaves and under the sod
There lurks a ripe fruit which the reapers have not gathered
The true harvest of the year—the boreal fruit
Which it bears forever,
With fondness annually watering and maturing it.
But man never severs the stalk
Which bears this palatable fruit.

THE MOON

Time wears her not; she doth his chariot guide;
  Mortality below her orb is placed.
                    RALEIGH

The full-orbed moon with unchanged ray
  Mounts up the eastern sky,
Not doomed to these short nights for aye,
  But shining steadily.

She does not wane, but my fortune,
  Which her rays do not bless,
My wayward path declineth soon,
  But she shines not the less.

And if she faintly glimmers here,
  And paled is her light,
Yet alway in her proper sphere
  She's mistress of the night.

As there is contention among the fishermen who shall be the first to reach the pond as soon as the ice will bear, in spite of the cold, as the hunters are forward to take the field as soon as the first snow has fallen, so the observer, or he who would make the most of his life for discipline, must be abroad early and late, in spite of cold and wet, in pursuit of nobler game, whose traces are then most distinct. A life which, pursued, does not earth itself, does not burrow downward but upward, which takes not to the trees but to the heavens as its home, which the hunter pursues with winged thoughts and aspirations,—these the dogs that tree it,—rallying his pack with the bugle notes of undying faith, and returns with some worthier trophy than a fox's tail, a life we seek, not to destroy it, but to save our own.

Journal, January 1, 1854

I AM BOUND, I AM BOUND, FOR A DISTANT SHORE

I am bound, I am bound, for a distant shore,
By a lonely isle, by a far Azore,
There it is, there it is, the treasure I seek,
On the barren sands of a desolate creek.

I come to my solitary woodland walk as the homesick go home. I thus dispose of the superfluous and see things as they really are, grand and beautiful. I have told many that I walk every day about half the daylight, but I think they do not believe it. I wish to get the Concord, the Massachusetts, the America, out of my head and be sane a part of every day. If there are missionaries for the heathen, why not send them to me? I wish to know something; I wish to be made better. I wish to forget, a considerable part of every day, all mean, narrow, trivial men (and this requires usually to forego and forget all personal relations so long), and therefore I come out to these solitudes, where the problem of existence is simplified. I get away a mile or two from the town into the stillness and solitude of nature, with rocks, trees, weeds, snow about me. I enter some glade in the woods, perchance, where a few weeds and dry leaves alone lift themselves above the surface of the snow, and it is as if I had come to an open window. . . . It is as if I always met in those places some grand, serene, immortal, infinitely encouraging, though invisible, companion, and walked with him.

Journal, January 7, 1857

Standing quite alone, far in the forest, while the wind is shaking down snow from the trees, and leaving the only human tracks behind us, we find our reflections of a richer variety than the life of cities. The chickadee and nuthatch are more inspiring society than statesmen and philosophers, and we shall return to these last as to more vulgar companions. In this lonely glen, with its brook draining the slopes, its creased ice and crystals of all hues, where the spruces and hemlocks stand up on either side, and the rush and sere wild oats in the rivulet itself, our lives are more serene and worthy to contemplate.

"A Winter Walk"

THE CHICADEE

The chicadee
Hops near to me.

There is a vale which none hath seen,
Where foot of man has never been,
Such as here lives with toil and strife,
An anxious and a sinful life.

There every virtue has its birth,
Ere it descends upon the earth,
And thither every deed returns,
Which in the generous bosom burns.

There love is warm, and youth is young,
And poetry is yet unsung,
For Virtue still adventures there,
And freely breathes her native air.

And ever, if you hearken well,
You still may hear its vesper bell,
And tread of high-souled men go by,
Their thoughts conversing with the sky.

One hastens to southern Africa to chase the giraffe; but surely that is not the game he would be after. How long, pray, would a man hunt giraffes if he could? Snipes and woodcocks also may afford rare sport; but I trust it would be nobler game to shoot one's self.—

> "Direct your eye right inward, and you'll find
> A thousand regions in your mind
> Yet undiscovered. Travel them, and be
> Expert in home-cosmography."

What does Africa,—what does the West stand for? Is not our own interior white on the chart? black though it may prove, like the coast, when discovered. . . . Be rather the Mungo Park, the Lewis and Clark and Frobisher, of your own streams and oceans; explore your own higher latitudes,—with shiploads of preserved meats to support you, if they be necessary; and pile the empty cans sky-high for a sign.

Walden, "Conclusion"

THE VIRGIN

With her calm, aspiring eyes
She doth tempt the earth to rise,
With humility over all,
She doth tempt the sky to fall.

In her place she still doth stand
A pattern unto the firm land
While revolving spheres come round
To embrace her stable ground.

I said to myself,—I said to others,—"There comes into my mind such an indescribable, infinite, all-absorbing, divine, heavenly pleasure, a sense of elevation and expansion, and [I] have had nought to do with it. I perceive that I am dealt with by superior powers. This is a pleasure, a joy, an existence which I have not procured myself. I speak as a witness on the stand, and tell what I have perceived." The morning and the evening were sweet to me, and I led a life aloof from society of men. I wondered if a mortal had ever known what I knew. I looked in books for some recognition of a kindred experience, but, strange to say, I found none. Indeed, I was slow to discover that other men had had this experience, for it had been possible to read books and to associate with men on other grounds. The maker of me was improving me. When I detected this interference I was profoundly moved. For years I marched as to a music in comparison with which the military music of the streets is noise and discord. I was daily intoxicated, and yet no man could call me intemperate. With all your science can you tell how it is, and whence it is, that light comes into the soul?

Journal, July 16, 1851

I sailed up a river with a pleasant wind,
New lands, new people, and new thoughts to find;
Many fair reaches and headlands appeared,
And many dangers were there to be feared;
But when I remember where I have been,
And the fair landscapes that I have seen,
THOU seemest the only permanent shore,
The cape never rounded, nor wandered o'er.

I have read in a Hindoo book, that "there was a king's son, who, being expelled in infancy from his native city, was brought up by a forester, and, growing up to maturity in that state, imagined himself to belong to the barbarous race with which he lived. One of his father's ministers having discovered him, revealed to him what he was, and the misconception of his character was removed, and he knew himself to be a prince. So soul," continues the Hindoo philosopher, "from the circumstances in which it is placed, mistakes its own character, until the truth is revealed to it by some holy teacher, and then it knows itself to be *Brahme*."

Walden, "Where I Lived, and What I Lived For"

The snow is the great betrayer. It not only shows the tracks of mice, otters, etc., etc., which else we should rarely if ever see, but the tree sparrows are more plainly seen against its white ground, and they in turn are attracted by the dark weeds which it reveals. . . . Why do the vast snow plains give us pleasure, the twilight of the bent and half-buried woods? Is not all there consonant with virtue, justice, purity, courage, magnanimity? Are we not cheered by the sight? And does not all this amount to the track of a higher life than the otter's, a life which has not gone by and left a footprint merely, but is there with its beauty, its music, its perfume, its sweetness, to exhilarate and recreate us? Where there is a perfect government of the world according to the highest laws, is there no trace of intelligence there, whether in the snow or the earth, or in ourselves? No other trail but such as a dog can smell? Is there none which an angel can detect and follow? None to guide a man on his pilgrimage, which water will not conceal? Is there no odor of sanctity to be perceived? Is its trail too old? Have mortals lost the scent?

Journal, January 1, 1854

It appears to me that, to one standing on the heights of philosophy, mankind and the works of man will have sunk out of sight altogether; that man is altogether too much insisted on. The poet says the proper study of mankind is man. I say, study to forget all that; take wider views of the universe. . . . In order to avoid delusions, I would fain let man go by and behold a universe in which man is but as a grain of sand. I am sure that those of my thoughts which consist, or are contemporaneous, with social personal connections, however humane, are not the wisest and widest, most universal. What is the village, city, State, nation, aye the civilized world, that it should concern a man so much? the thought of them affects me in my wisest hours as when I pass a woodchuck's hole. It is a comfortable place to nestle, no doubt, and we have friends, some sympathizing ones, it may be, and a hearth, there; but I have only to get up at midnight, aye to soar or wander a little in my thought by day, to find them all slumbering. . . .

I do not value any view of the universe into which man and the institutions of man enter very largely and absorb much of the attention. Man is but the place where I stand, and the prospect hence is infinite. It is not a chamber of mirrors which reflect me. When I reflect, I find that there is other than me. Man is past phenomenon to philosophy. The universe is larger than enough for man's abode. Some rarely go outdoors, most are always at home at night, very few indeed have stayed out all night once in their lives, fewer still have gone behind the world of humanity, seen its institutions like toadstools by the wayside.

Journal, April 2, 1852

THE ATLANTIDES

The smothered streams of love, which flow
More bright than Phlegethon, more low,
Island us ever, like the sea,
In an Atlantic mystery.
Our fabled shores none ever reach,
No mariner has found our beach,
Scarcely our mirage now is seen,
And neighboring waves with floating green,
Yet still the oldest charts contain
Some dotted outline of our main;
In ancient times midsummer days
Unto the western islands' gaze,
To Teneriffe and the Azores,
Have shown our faint and cloud-like shores.

But sink not yet, ye desolate isles,
Anon your coast with commerce smiles,
And richer freights ye'll furnish far
Than Africa or Malabar.
Be fair, be fertile evermore,
Ye rumored but untrodden shore,
Princes and monarchs will contend
Who first unto your land shall send,
And pawn the jewels of the crown
To call your distant soil their own.

We hug the earth,—how rarely we mount! Methinks we might elevate ourselves a little more. We might climb a tree, at least. I found my account in climbing a tree once. It was a tall white-pine, on the top of a hill; and though I got well pitched, I was well paid for it, for I discovered new mountains in the horizon which I had never seen before,—so much more of the earth and the heavens. I might have walked about the foot of the tree for three-score years and ten, and yet I certainly should never have seen them. But, above all, I discovered around me,—it was near the end of June,—on the ends of the topmost branches only, a few minute and delicate red cone-like blossoms, the fertile flower of the white pine looking heavenward. I carried straightway to the village the topmost spire, and showed it to stranger jurymen who walked the streets,—for it was court-week,—and the farmers and lumber-dealers and wood-choppers and hunters, and not one had ever seen the like before, but they wondered as at a star dropped down. Tell of ancient architects finishing their works on the tops of columns as perfectly as on the lower and more visible parts! Nature has from the first expanded the minute blossoms of the forest only toward the heavens, above men's heads and unobserved by them. We see only the flowers that are under our feet in the meadows. The pines have developed their delicate blossoms on the highest twigs of the wood every summer for ages, as well over the heads of Nature's red children as of her white ones; yet scarcely a farmer or hunter in the land has ever seen them.

"Walking"

PART TWO

The Habit of Living Meanly

A GREAT IDEA is a useful invention, like an eyeglass or a new fuel. A doctrine may be a piece of charcoal left behind by an earlier genius for a token of remembrance, as Whitman said, "designedly dropped," and useful now in our daily lives. When an idea is an eyeglass, details otherwise fuzzy become sharp.

Thoreau understands that we have a winged life inside us, even if people are presently using us as a table. When Thoreau set that idea to his eyes, he saw that most people around him were living meanly.

We hate it when observers notice mean lives, because we are afraid we may be among those being watched. Much of the hostility to Thoreau, which I remember feeling strongly in college—scribbled insults in the margins of my *Walden* remain as testimony—comes from the fear that we are being watched.

What is it to live meanly? We may easily confuse living a mean life with living a low life. Puritan Christians struggled against a low life, which to them meant giving in to instinctual urges, but in Thoreau's understanding, many Puritans nevertheless lived mean lives. And the twelfth-century Chinese Taoists—mad about sex, some of them—remind us that though we may spend hours each day balancing yang and yin, we can still live meanly. It isn't a matter of living our sexuality or avoiding it, of embodying animal instincts or rising above them, of eating huge dinners or not eating them. Living meanly, to Thoreau, is the opposite of "living sincerely." To live sincerely is to live your own life, not your father's life or your mother's life or your neighbor's life; to spend soul on large concerns, not to waste your life as a kind of human ant carrying around small burdens; and finally, to live sincerely is to "live deep and suck out all the marrow of life," as Thoreau declares in *Walden*. That may require unsociability. Thoreau noticed that at a certain age boys remain in shadows and corners of rooms, look a little wild, make up their minds about a given grownup in a second, and may come to supper or not. Thoreau values that unsociability in both boys and girls. But those moments soon disappear, replaced by an old anxiety to please.

Many women have described the moment when they realized to their dismay that they had spent their lives trying to please others. They had tuned themselves to others' needs while ignoring their own. And men do the same thing wholesale, so to speak; instead of retailing their attention to particular persons, they try to guess the needs of entire generations or congregations, and so end up leading their congregation's life, or their generation's life.

The ancient metaphor for living meanly is sleep. Lovers and writers can be asleep. "A man can make war in his sleep, make love in his sleep, even write books in his sleep, but they will only serve to put other people to sleep." This, a parable that Gurdjieff heard as a youth, would have delighted Thoreau. The state of being awake could then be called "living sincerely." Thoreau's wit is just as sharp as the parable maker's when in the opening passage of *Walden* he says, "Moreover, I, on my side, require of every writer, first or last, a simple and sincere account of his own life, and not merely what he has heard of other men's lives; some such account as he would send to his kindred from a distant land; for if he has lived sincerely, it must have been in a distant land to me."

That is the first sentence of Thoreau's that I ever memorized, and I still admire it. At the sentence's end the claws come out, and we realize that though Henry David Thoreau is called a transcendentalist, he has not "transcended his negative emotions," as some New Age transcendentalists long to do; on the contrary, he often expresses anger, contempt and disdain. He stings the unwary. He distinguishes the shallow life from the deep and does not tolerate people who live shallowly.

In our century, Rainer Maria Rilke has written a number of poems that distinguish between his hurried life on the one hand and his deep life on the other. This poem of his is from *Das Stundenbuch*:

> *My life is not this steeply sloping hour,*
> *in which you see me hurrying.*
> *Much stands behind me; I stand before it like a tree.*
> *I am only one of my many mouths,*
> *and at that, the one that will be still the soonest.*

I am the rest between two notes,
which are somehow always in discord
because Death's note wants to climb over—
but in the dark interval, reconciled,
they stay there, trembling.
                    And the song goes on, beautiful.

This is how Thoreau said it in prose:

I love to weigh, to settle, to gravitate toward that which most strongly and rightfully attracts
me;—not hang by the beam of the scale and try to weigh less,—not suppose a case, but take the
case that is; to travel the only path I can, and that on which no power can resist me. It affords
me no satisfaction to commence to spring an arch before I have got a solid foundation. Let us not
play at kittly-benders. There is a solid bottom everywhere. We read that the traveller asked the
boy if the swamp before him had a hard bottom. The boy replied that it had. But presently the
traveller's horse sank in up to the girths, and he observed to the boy, "I thought you said that
this bog had a hard bottom.". "So it has," answered the latter, "but you have not got half way
to it yet." (Walden)

Thoreau does not expect that the "sleep" will end today or tomorrow, but he
has some hope. It is not clear that nature wants men and women to wake: perhaps
nature prefers them to remain asleep, work like oxen or blind mules and then lie
down beneath the ground. Thoreau develops a pun around the word "sleepers,"
which is commonly used for railway ties: "We do not ride on the railroad; it rides
upon us. Did you ever think what those sleepers are that underlie the railroad?
Each one is a man, an Irishman, or a Yankee man. . . . I am glad to know that it takes
a gang of men for every five miles to keep the sleepers down and level in their beds
as it is, for this is a sign that they may sometime get up again."

Thoreau's hope that he may escape such sleep turns into wit, and his fear that
he cannot escape it turns into a generalized sorrow such as we hear in the Babylonian
epic *Gilgamesh* or in ancient Egyptian laments. He notices how easy it is for us to
sentimentalize a trail of smoke rising from a valley farmhouse:

It suggests all of domestic felicity beneath. . . . When I look down on that roof I am not reminded
of the mortgage which the village bank has on that property,—that that family long since sold
itself to the devil and wrote the deed with their blood. I am not reminded that the old man I see
in the yard is one who has lived beyond his calculated time, whom the young one is merely

"carrying through" in fulfillment of his contract; that the man at the pump is watering the milk. I am not reminded of the idiot that sits by the kitchen fire. (Journal, *October 3, 1859*)

The suffering that the citizens of Concord go through when living meanly or asleep struck Thoreau as Oriental in its fierceness: "What I have heard of Bramins sitting exposed to four fires and looking in the face of the sun; or hanging suspended, with their heads downward, over flames; . . . or measuring with their bodies, like caterpillars, the breadth of vast empires; or standing on one leg on the tops of pillars—even these forms of conscious penance are hardly more incredible and astonishing than the scenes which I daily witness."

He feels grief for the life wasted around him. The larvae of the Plicipennes, he mentions, eventually will leave "their sunken habitations, and, crawling up the stems of plants, or to the surface, like gnats, as perfect insects henceforth, flutter over the surface of the water, or sacrifice their short lives in the flames of our candles at evening." His grief can lead him to marvelously agile leaps of language, as when he asks why we should "level downward to our dullest perception always, and praise that as common sense? The commonest sense is the sense of men asleep, which they express by snoring."

Thoreau's awareness of the suffering entailed in "living insincerely" commits him to create sentences athletic and daring enough to be worthy of his own nature, and the reader will find a number of these wiry sentences, both in prose texts and in poems here.

Among the signs of autumn I perceive
The Roman wormwood (called by learned men
Ambrosia elatior, food for gods,—
For to impartial science the humblest weed
Is as immortal once as the proudest flower—)
Sprinkles its yellow dust over my shoes
As I cross the now neglected garden
—We trample under foot the food of gods
& spill their nectar in each drop of dew—
My honest shoes Fast friends that never stray
Far from my couch thus powdered countryfied
Bearing many a mile the marks of their adventure
At the post-house disgrace the Gallic gloss
Of those well dressed ones who no morning dew
Nor Roman wormwood ever have been through
Who never walk but are *transported* rather—
For what old crime of theirs I do not gather.

It would surpass the powers of a well man nowadays to take up his bed and walk, and I should certainly advise a sick one to lay down his bed and run. When I have met an immigrant tottering under a bundle which contained his all,—looking like an enormous wen which had grown out of the nape of his neck,—I have pitied him, not because that was his all, but because he had all *that* to carry. If I have got to drag my trap, I will take care that it be a light one and do not nip me in a vital part. But perchance it would be wisest never to put one's paw into it.

Walden, "Economy"

I make ye an offer,
Ye gods, hear the scoffer,
The scheme will not hurt you,
If ye will find goodness, I will find virtue.
Though I am your creature,
And child of your nature,
I have pride still unbended,
And blood undescended,
Some free independence,
And my own descendants.
I cannot toil blindly,
Though ye behave kindly,
And I swear by the rood,
I'll be slave to no God.
If ye will deal plainly,
I will strive mainly,
If ye will discover,
Great plans to your lover,
And give him a sphere
Somewhat larger than here.

One day, when my axe had come off and I had cut a green hickory for a wedge, driving it with a stone, and had placed the whole to soak in a pond-hole in order to swell the wood, I saw a striped snake run into the water, and he lay on the bottom, apparently without inconvenience, as long as I stayed there, or more than a quarter of an hour; perhaps because he had not yet fairly come out of the torpid state. It appeared to me that for a like reason men remain in their present low and primitive condition; but if they should feel the influence of the spring of springs arousing them, they would of necessity rise to a higher and more ethereal life. I had previously seen the snakes in frosty mornings in my path with portions of their bodies still numb and inflexible, waiting for the sun to thaw them. On the 1st of April it rained and melted the ice, and in the early part of the day, which was very foggy, I heard a stray goose groping about over the pond and cackling as if lost, or like the spirit of the fog.

Walden, "Economy"

Sometimes I heard the foxes as they ranged over the snow-crust, in moonlight nights, in search of a partridge or other game, barking raggedly and demonically like forest dogs, as if laboring with some anxiety, or seeking expression, struggling for light and to be dogs outright and run freely in the streets; for if we take the ages into our account, may there not be a civilization going on among brutes as well as men? They seemed to me to be rudimental, burrowing men, still standing on their defence, awaiting their transformation.

Walden, "Winter Animals"

I have travelled a good deal in Concord; and everywhere, in shops, and offices, and fields, the inhabitants have appeared to me to be doing penance in a thousand remarkable ways. What I have heard of Bramins sitting exposed to four fires and looking in the face of the sun; or hanging suspended, with their heads downward, over flames; or looking at the heavens over their shoulders "until it becomes impossible for them to resume their natural position, while from the twist of the neck nothing but liquids can pass into the stomach;" or dwelling, chained for life, at the foot of a tree; or measuring with their bodies, like caterpillars, the breadth of vast empires; or standing on one leg on the tops of pillars—even these forms of conscious penance are hardly more incredible and astonishing than the scenes which I daily witness.

Walden, "Economy"

Between the traveller and the setting sun,
Upon some drifting sand heap of the shore,
A hound stands o'er the carcass of a man.

I see young men, my townsmen, whose misfortune it is to have inherited farms, houses, barns, cattle, and farming tools; for these are more easily acquired than got rid of. Better if they had been born in the open pasture and suckled by a wolf, that they might have seen with clearer eyes what field they were called to labor in. Who made them serfs of the soil? Why should they eat their sixty acres, when man is condemned to eat only his peck of dirt? Why should they begin digging their graves as soon as they are born? They have got to live a man's life, pushing all these things before them, and get on as well as they can. How many a poor immortal soul have I met well-nigh crushed and smothered under its load, creeping down the road of life, pushing before it a barn seventy-five feet by forty, its Augean stables never cleansed, and one hundred acres of land, tillage, mowing, pasture, and wood-lot!

Walden, "Economy"

Still we live meanly, like ants; though the fable tells us that we were long ago changed into men; like pygmies we fight with cranes; it is error upon error, and clout upon clout, and our best virtue has for its occasion a superfluous and evitable wretchedness. Our life is frittered away by detail. An honest man has hardly need to count more than his ten fingers, or in extreme cases he may add his ten toes, and lump the rest. Simplicity, simplicity, simplicity! I say, let your affairs be as two or three, and not a hundred or a thousand; instead of a million count half a dozen, and keep your accounts on your thumb-nail. In the midst of this chopping sea of civilized life, such are the clouds and storms and quicksands and thousand-and-one items to be allowed for, that a man has to live, if he would not founder and go to the bottom and not make his port at all, by dead reckoning, and he must be a great calculator indeed who succeeds. Simplify, simplify. Instead of three meals a day, if it be necessary eat but one; instead of a hundred dishes, five, and reduce other things in proportion. Our life is like a German Confederacy, made up of petty states, with its boundary forever fluctuating, so that even a German cannot tell you how it is bounded at any moment.

Walden, "Where I Lived, and What I Lived For"

I'm thankful that my life doth not deceive
Itself with a low loftiness, half height,
And think it soars when still it dip[s] its way
Beneath the clouds on noiseless pinion
Like the crow or owl, but it doth know
The full extent of all its trivialness,
Compared with the splendid heights above.
See how it waits to watch the mail come in
While 'hind its back *the sun goes out perchance.*
And yet their lumbering cart brings me no word
Not one scrawled leaf such as my neighbors get
To cheer them with the slight events forsooth
Faint ups and downs of their far distant friends—
And now tis passed. What next? See the long train
Of teams wreathed in dust, their atmosphere;
Shall I attend until the last is passed?
Else why these ears that hear the leader's bells
Or eyes that link me in procession?
But hark! the drowsy day has done its task,
Far in yon hazy field where stands a barn
Unanxious hens improve the sultry hour
And with contented voice now brag their deed—
A new laid egg—Now let the day decline—
They'll lay another by tomorrow's sun.

This world is a place of business. What an infinite bustle! I am awaked almost every night by the panting of the locomotive. It interrupts my dreams. There is no sabbath. It would be glorious to see mankind at leisure for once. It is nothing but work, work, work. I cannot easily buy a blank-book to write thoughts in; they are commonly ruled for dollars and cents. An Irishman, seeing me making a minute in the fields, took it for granted that I was calculating my wages. If a man was tossed out of a window when an infant, and so made a cripple for life, or scared out of his wits by the Indians, it is regretted chiefly because he was thus incapacitated for— business! I think that there is nothing, not even crime, more opposed to poetry, to philosophy, ay, to life itself, than this incessant business.

"Life Without Principle"

The mass of men lead lives of quiet desperation. What is called resignation is confirmed desperation. From the desperate city you go into the desperate country, and have to console yourselves with the bravery of minks and muskrats. A stereotyped but unconscious despair is concealed even under what are called the games and amusements of mankind. There is no play in them, for this comes after work.

Walden, "Economy"

Why should we live with such hurry and waste of life? We are determined to be starved before we are hungry. Men say that a stitch in time saves nine, and so they take a thousand stitches to-day to save nine tomorrow. As for *work*, we haven't any of any consequence. We have the Saint Vitus' dance, and cannot possibly keep our heads still. If I should only give a few pulls at the parish bell-rope, as for a fire, that is, without setting the bell, there is hardly a man on his farm in the outskirts of Concord, notwithstanding that press of engagements which was his excuse so many times this morning, nor a boy, nor a woman, I might almost say, but would forsake all and follow that sound, not mainly to save property from the flames, but, if we will confess the truth, much more to see it burn, since burn it must, and we, be it known, did not set it on fire,—or to see it put out, and have a hand in it, if that is done as handsomely; yes, even if it were the parish church itself. Hardly a man takes a half-hour's nap after dinner, but when he wakes he holds up his head and asks, "What's the news?" as if the rest of mankind had stood his sentinels. Some give directions to be waked every half-hour, doubtless for no other purpose; and then, to pay for it, they tell what they have dreamed. After a night's sleep the news is as indispensable as the breakfast. "Pray tell me anything new that has happened to a man anywhere on this globe,"—and he reads it over his coffee and rolls, that a man has had his eyes gouged out this morning on the Wachito River; never dreaming the while that he lives in the dark unfathomed mammoth cave of this world, and has but the rudiment of an eye himself.

Walden, "Where I Lived, and What I Lived For"

The way in which men cling to old institutions after the life has departed out of them, and out of themselves, reminds me of those monkeys which cling by their tails,—aye, whose tails contract about the limbs, even the dead limbs, of the forest, and they hang suspended beyond the hunter's reach long after they are dead. It is of no use to argue with such men. They have not an apprehensive intellect, but merely, as it were, a prehensile tail. . . . The tail itself contracts around the dead limb even after they themselves are dead, and not till sensible corruption takes place do they fall.

Journal, August 19, 1851

If we do not get out sleepers, and forge rails, and devote days and nights to the work, but go to tinkering upon our *lives* to improve *them*, who will build railroads? And if railroads are not built, how shall we get to heaven in season? But if we stay at home and mind our business, who will want railroads? We do not ride on the railroad; it rides upon us. Did you ever think what those sleepers are that underlie the railroad? Each one is a man, an Irishman, or a Yankee man. The rails are laid on them, and they are covered with sand, and the cars run smoothly over them. They are sound sleepers, I assure you. And every few years a new lot is laid down and run over; so that, if some have the pleasure of riding on a rail, others have the misfortune to be ridden upon. And when they run over a man that is walking in his sleep, a supernumerary sleeper in the wrong position, and wake him up, they suddenly stop the cars, and make a hue and cry about it, as if this were an exception. I am glad to know that it takes a gang of men for every five miles to keep the sleepers down and level in their beds as it is, for this is a sign that they may sometime get up again.

Walden, "Where I Lived, and What I Lived For"

Though all the fates should prove unkind,
Leave not your native land behind.
The ship, becalmed, at length stands still;
The steed must rest beneath the hill;
But swiftly still our fortunes pace
To find us out in every place.

The vessel, though her masts be firm,
Beneath her copper bears a worm;
Around the cape, across the line,
Till fields of ice her course confine;
It matters not how smooth the breeze,
How shallow or how deep the seas,
Whether she bears Manilla twine,
Or in her hold Madeira wine,
Or China teas, or Spanish hides,
In port or quarantine she rides;
Far from New England's blustering shore,
New England's worm her hulk shall bore,
And sink her in the Indian seas,
Twine, wine, and hides, and China teas.

Men have an indistinct notion that if they keep up this activity of joint stocks and spades long enough all will at length ride somewhere, in next to no time, and for nothing; but though a crowd rushes to the depot, and the conductor shouts "All aboard!" when the smoke is blown away and the vapor condensed, it will be perceived that a few are riding,—but the rest are run over—and it will be called, and will be, "A melancholy accident."

Walden, "Economy"

Stretched over the brooks, in the midst of the frost-bound meadows, we may observe the submarine cottages of the caddis-worms, the larvae of the Plicipennes; their small cylindrical cases built around themselves, composed of flags, sticks, grass, and withered leaves, shells, and pebbles, in form and color like the wrecks which strew the bottom,—now drifting along over the pebbly bottom, now whirling in tiny eddies and dashing down steep falls, or sweeping rapidly along with the current, or else swaying to and fro at the end of some grass-blade or root. Anon they will leave their sunken habitations, and, crawling up the stems of plants, or to the surface, like gnats, as perfect insects henceforth, flutter over the surface of the water, or sacrifice their short lives in the flame of our candles at evening.

"A Winter Walk"

Why level downward to our dullest perception always, and praise that as common sense? The commonest sense is the sense of men asleep, which they express by snoring. Sometimes we are inclined to class those who are once-and-a-half-witted with the half-witted, because we appreciate only a third part of their wit. Some would find fault with the morning red, if they ever got up early enough. "They pretend," as I hear, "that the verses of Kabir have four different senses; illusion, spirit, intellect, and the exoteric doctrine of the Vedas;" but in this part of the world it is considered a ground for complaint if a man's writings admit of more than one interpretation. While England endeavors to cure the potato-rot, will not any endeavor to cure the brain-rot, which prevails so much more widely and fatally?

Walden, "Conclusion"

As I stand under the hill beyond J. Hosmer's and look over the plains westward toward Acton and see the farmhouses nearly half a mile apart, few and solitary, in these great fields between these stretching woods, out of the world, where the children have to go far to school; the still, stagnant, heart-eating, life-everlasting, and gone-to-seed country, so far from the post-office where the weekly paper comes, wherein the new-married wife cannot live for loneliness, and the young man has to depend upon his horse for society; see young J. Hosmer's house, whither he returns with his wife in despair after living in the city,—I standing in Tarbell's road, which he alone cannot break out,—the world in winter for most walkers reduced to a sled track winding far through the drifts, all springs sealed up and no digressions; where the old man thinks he may possibly afford to rust it out, not having long to live, but the young man pines to get nearer the post-office and the Lyceum, is restless and resolves to go to California, because the depot is a mile off (he hears the rattle of the cars at a distance and thinks the world is going by and leaving him); where rabbits and partridges multiply, and muskrats are more numerous than ever, and none of the farmer's sons are willing to be farmers, and the apple trees are decayed, and the cellar-holes are more numerous than the houses, and the rails are covered with lichens, and the old maids wish to sell out and move into the village, and have waited twenty years in vain for this purpose and never finished but one room in the house, never plastered nor painted, inside or out . . . where some men's breaths smell of rum, having smuggled in a jugful to alleviate their misery and solitude; where the owls give a regular serenade;—I say, standing there and seeing these things, I cannot realize that this is that hopeful young America which is famous throughout the world for its activity and enterprise, and this is the most thickly settled and Yankee part of it. What must be the condition of the *old* world!

Journal, January 27, 1852

John Farmer sat at his door one September evening, after a hard day's work, his mind still running on his labor more or less. Having bathed, he sat down to re-create his intellectual man. It was a rather cool evening, and some of his neighbors were apprehending a frost. He had not attended to the train of his thoughts long when he heard some one playing on a flute, and that sound harmonized with his mood. Still he thought of his work; but the burden of his thought was, that though this kept running in his head, and he found himself planning and contriving it against his will, yet it concerned him very little. It was no more than the scurf of his skin, which was constantly shuffled off. But the notes of the flute came home to his ears out of a different sphere from that he worked in, and suggested work for certain faculties which slumbered in him. They gently did away with the street, and the village, and the state in which he lived. A voice said to him,—Why do you stay here and live this mean moiling life, when a glorious existence is possible for you? Those same stars twinkle over other fields than these.—But how to come out of this condition and actually migrate thither? All that he could think of was to practise some new austerity, to let his mind descend into his body and redeem it, and treat himself with ever increasing respect.

Walden, "Higher Laws"

PART THREE

Going the Long Way Round

THOREAU'S MAJOR DECISION was his decision not to live meanly. The salt of this decision buoyed him up, floated him almost to the end of his life. It was daring because his father lived meanly, and probably his mother too. It was one thing for Yeats to decide on the lofty life of artistic poverty when he saw his father pursuing a similar life, and it was another thing for Thoreau to do so; for by doing so, Thoreau was acting the rebellious son. And that is dangerous.

Thoreau saw early on, in his poem "Though All the Fates Should Prove Unkind," that his own ship would sink. We can't say what the "worm" is that eats the hull, but we should not rule out his guilt over rebellion. The ship embarks, as Thoreau says, with flags raised, and cuts through the water jauntily, but what if, underneath the copper sheathing, a worm is eating at the wooden vessel?

> *Whether she bears Manilla twine,*
> *Or in her hold Madeira wine,*
> *Or China teas, or Spanish hides,*
> *In port or quarantine she rides;*
> *Far from New England's blustering shore,*
> *New England's worm her hulk shall bore,*
> *And sink her in the Indian seas,*
> *Twine, wine, and hides, and China teas.*

I feel that Thoreau's decision to leave his father's way of life was a complicated move, with something careful in it and something reckless, something noble and something destructive. But when he determined on it, he made sure that all of Concord knew, to cut off possibility of retreat.

The radiance that comes from that complicated, ambivalent decision makes the prose of *Walden* shine; the sentences glow with the heat given off by high spirits. If a book is a house, then, as Thoreau might say, the spirits of dried hickory and of a man who is in the right heat a house well.

Thoreau wanted greatness, and he wanted to live greatly, but most of all he wanted not to live meanly. Others have left a record of their decision not to live meanly—I think of Kierkegaard, Juan Ramón Jiménez, Emily Dickinson, Walt Whitman and Robert Frost—but none, I think, have seen so clearly, grasped so keenly, or defended so tenaciously the waiting period that such a decision entails. Agreeing to a waiting period is a part of it.

Jung remarks in one of his essays that some plants grow best out of direct sun, in damp light, or in northern light. When a man or woman determines to leap over the petty life and tries to hatch the egg dormant in the apple wood, he or she needs leisure time, and the courage to take it. Courage is needed to withstand the melancholy and loneliness. He or she learns that for years nothing tangible will come from this inward and invisible swerving. No fruit will appear that his or her family or the surrounding society can eat. Milton describes the grief beautifully in this sonnet:

> How soon hath Time, the subtle thief of youth,
>   Stol'n on his wing my three and twentieth year!
>   My hasting days fly on with full career,
>   But my late spring no bud or blossom shew'th.
> Perhaps my semblance might deceive the truth,
>   That I to manhood am arrived so near,
>   And inward ripeness doth much less appear,
>   That some more timely-happy spirits endu'th.
> Yet be it less or more, or soon or slow,
>   It shall be still in strictest measure ev'n,
>   To that same lot, however mean or high,
> Toward which Time leads me, and the will of Heav'n;
>   All is, if I have grace to use it so,
>   As ever in my great Task-Master's eye.

Thoreau, at twenty-five, writes in his journal (March 22, 1842): "Nothing can be more useful to a man than a determination not to be hurried." Richard Lebeaux, in his book *Young Man Thoreau*, pays attention to Thoreau's moratorium, adopting a term suggested by Erik Erikson. It took tremendous courage for Thoreau to refuse his town's insistence that he take a job the day after college graduation; there was no place in his townsmen's psyche for the man who waits. Thoreau's ability to endure a moratorium goes to the root of his courage and his accomplishment. He had to agree to change from a rooster to a setting hen, and he asked himself in his journal on March 26, 1842: "Are setting hens troubled with ennui? Nature is very kind; does she let them reflect? These long March days, setting on and on in the crevice of a hayloft, with no active employment! Do setting hens sleep?"

At other times Thoreau adopts the image of moulting: "Our moulting season, like that of the fowls, must be a crisis in our lives. The loon retires to solitary ponds to spend it. Thus also the snake casts its slough, and the caterpillar its wormy coat, by an internal industry and expansion; for clothes are but our outmost cuticle and mortal coil. Otherwise we shall be found sailing under false colors, and be inevitably cashiered at last by our own opinion, as well as that of mankind." (*Walden*)

Erikson observed the value of such a waiting period in the lives of Martin Luther and Gandhi. It is possible that at an earlier time initiation groups, made up of older men or older women, gave the young ones permission for a waiting period. Now each person has to demand, create and defend his or her own. I feel that Thoreau's declaration of the need for a moratorium is his greatest gift to the young. He does not require that each of us go, as he did, to the woods to live alone, as the Basques, Buddhists and some Native American cultures still do:

I would not have any one adopt my *mode of living on any account; for, besides that before he has fairly learned it I may have found out another for myself, I desire that there be as many different persons in the world as possible; but I would have each one be very careful to find out and pursue* his own *way, and not his father's or his mother's or his neighbor's instead.* (Walden)

But he asks each person to take time early in life for a moratorium, even if only two years. In *Walden* he asks the community members who have read his words to encourage and support their young people in this effort, and testifies to its value:

Sometimes . . . I sat in my sunny doorway from sunrise till noon, rapt in a revery, amidst the pines and hickories and sumachs. . . . I grew in those seasons like corn in the night.

Thoreau's own moratorium was long. He began it tentatively in 1837, when he was twenty, on graduating from Harvard. The next year he and his brother John established a small school, where both taught for three years. When John became ill, and the brothers dissolved the school, Henry's moratorium began in earnest. On his last day of teaching, Henry wrote a magnificent poem in four lines; after a dull, cloudy day the sun came out in late afternoon:

Methinks all things have travelled since you shined,
But only Time, and clouds, Time's team, have moved;
Again foul weather shall not change my mind,
But in the shade I will believe what in the sun I loved.

Seeing the faces of students respond, and receiving their affection and gratitude, resembles living in the sun. But Thoreau agrees to leave that sunlight and live in the shade, and he swears that "in the shade I will believe what in the sun I loved." It is an original and powerful line.

It took thirteen years after that day for *Walden* to appear in print; the book was published in 1854, only eight years before Thoreau died. Its appearance meant the end of his moratorium, and he wrote in his journal on September 19, 1854:

Thinking this afternoon of the prospect of my writing lectures and going abroad to read them the next winter, I realized how incomparably great the advantages of obscurity and poverty which I have enjoyed so long.... I have given myself up to nature; I have lived so many springs and summers and autumns and winters as if I had nothing else to do but live them, and imbibe whatever nutriment they had for me;... If I go abroad lecturing, how shall I ever recover the lost winter?

One could say that Thoreau had twenty-four years of youth, thirteen years of moratorium and eight years of arrival or visibility. We know from reading *Walden* that his waiting period bore fruit. That book has a gathered sweetness, a grounded-ness in every sentence, a psychic weight, as if each page were a chunk of maple. Robert Frost, in an introductory essay to his collected poems titled "The Figure a Poem Makes," said of a good poem: "Its most precious quality will remain its having run itself and carried away the poet with it. Read it a hundred times; it will forever keep its freshness as a metal keeps its fragrance." Thoreau kept his mouth shut until it was time to speak. Each sentence in *Walden* is bold, precise and calculated to arouse opposition: "From the desperate city you go into the desperate country, and have to console yourselves with the bravery of minks and muskrats." Each sentence is a stone, and he has consciously shaped edges on it before he puts it in your hand.

Thoreau loved malic acid, that pungent power in small wild apples. When we taste that acid, we know that no one engineered this fruit to please large numbers of people. So in his moratorium Thoreau learned to grow small wild apples. He was also able "to drive life into a corner, and reduce it to its lowest terms, and, if it proved to be mean, why then to get the whole and genuine meanness of it, and publish its meanness to the world; or if it were sublime, to know it by experience, and be able to give a true account of it in my next excursion." (*Walden*) He became acquainted with the night, with the sorrow of the woods and the melancholy of the snow; he found depths and learned to trust them; he lived alone and liked the company. Once a writer has had that experience, he is content to write for the few who understand him, rather than for the millions who might, with the help of a loudspeaker, hear him.

Thoreau made a tart distinction between hearing and understanding. He said, in *Walden*, "The orator yields to the inspiration of a transient occasion, and speaks to the mob before him, to those who can *hear* him; but the writer, whose more equable life is his occasion, and who would be distracted by the event and the crowd which inspire the orator, speaks to the intellect and heart of mankind, to all in any age who can *understand* him."

We can ask of every writer whether he or she is writing to be heard, or to be understood. One danger of large poetry readings in our time is that in them the poet is urged to speak to those who can hear; those who understand the poet may not yet be born.

Did the moratorium damage Thoreau? I would say that it increased his sense that he was superior to others, of which he already had too much, and it must have increased also the compensatory sense of inferiority. By omitting domestic love, wife, children and community position, he decreased the number of unknowns in his life, and perhaps the number of knowns. I also think his moratorium went on so long that he resigned himself to not being at home in either male or female company. On July 26, 1852, he wrote in his journal:

By my intimacy with nature I find myself withdrawn from man. My interest in the sun and the moon, in the morning and the evening, compels me to solitude.

The grandest picture in the world is the sunset sky. In your higher moods what man is there to meet? You are of necessity isolated. The mind that perceives clearly any natural beauty is in that instant withdrawn from human society. My desire for society is infinitely increased; my fitness for any actual society is diminished.

The poems and prose pieces in this section center on the decision Thoreau made to move away from the "lives of quiet desperation" and his thoughts about the waiting period that followed, the long time when "no bud or blossom sheweth." Some journal passages suggest the images that he used to nourish him at that period: images of the vivid life that goes on underneath the snow, the picture of a hibernating bear, the story of an artist in ancient India who "made no compromise with Time." One poem, "Among the Worst of Men That Ever Lived," hints at his pride that he had become one of those citizens of Concord and the world who, despite all the elevated talk of spirituality around him, and the availability of high-spirited horses able to clear "riders" or fence poles easily, took the slow way and "went on to heaven the long way round."

At midnight's hour I raised my head
The owls were seeking for their bread
The foxes barked impatient still
At their wan fate they bear so ill—
I thought me of eternities delayed
And of commands but half obeyed—
The night wind rustled through the glade
As if a force of men there staid
The word was whispered through the ranks
And every hero seized his lance
The word was whispered through the ranks
   Advance.

By poverty, *i.e.* simplicity of life and fewness of incidents, I am solidified and crystallized, as a vapor or liquid by cold. It is a singular concentration of strength and energy and flavor. Chastity is perpetual acquaintance with the All. My diffuse and vaporous life becomes as the frost leaves and spiculae radiant as gems on the weeds and stubble in a winter morning. You think that I am impoverishing myself by withdrawing from men, but in my solitude I have woven for myself a silken web or *chrysalis*, and, nymph-like, shall ere long burst forth a more perfect creature, fitted for a higher society. By simplicity, commonly called poverty, my life is concentrated and so becomes organized, or a κόσμος [cosmos], which before was inorganic and lumpish.

Journal, February 8, 1857

There were times when I could not afford to sacrifice the bloom of the present moment to any work, whether of the head or hands. I love a broad margin to my life. Sometimes, in a summer morning, having taken my accustomed bath, I sat in my sunny doorway from sunrise till noon, rapt in a revery, amidst the pines and hickories and sumachs, in undisturbed solitude and stillness, while the birds sang around or flitted noiseless through the house, until by the sun falling in at my west window, or the noise of some traveller's wagon on the distant highway, I was reminded of the lapse of time. I grew in those seasons like corn in the night, and they were far better than any work of the hands would have been. They were not time subtracted from my life, but so much over and above my usual allowance. I realized what the Orientals mean by contemplation and the forsaking of works. For the most part, I minded not how the hours went. The day advanced as if to light some work of mine; it was morning, and lo, now it is evening, and nothing memorable is accomplished. Instead of singing like the birds, I silently smiled at my incessant good fortune. As the sparrow had its trill, sitting on the hickory before my door, so had I my chuckle or suppressed warble which he might hear out of my nest.

Walden, "Sounds"

MANHOOD

I love to see the man, a long-lived child,
As yet uninjured by all worldly taint
As the fresh infant whose whole life is play.
'Tis a serene spectacle for a serene day;
But better still I love to contemplate
The mature soul of lesser innocence,
Who hath travelled far on life's dusty road
Far from the starting point of infancy
And proudly bears his small degen'racy
Blazon'd on his memorial standard high
Who from the sad experience of his fate
Since his bark struck on that unlucky rock
Has proudly steered his life with his own hands.
Though his face harbors less of innocence
Yet there do chiefly lurk within its depths
Furrowed by care, but yet all over spread
With the ripe bloom of a self-wrought content
Noble resolves which do reprove the gods
And it doth more assert man's eminence
Above the happy level of the brute
And more doth advertise me of the heights
To which no natural path doth ever lead
No natural light can ever light our steps,
—But the far-piercing ray that shines
From the recesses of a brave man's eye.

Why should we be in such desperate haste to succeed and in such desperate enterprises? If a man does not keep pace with his companions, perhaps it is because he hears a different drummer. Let him step to the music which he hears, however measured or far away. It is not important that he should mature as soon as an apple tree or an oak. Shall he turn his spring into summer?

Walden, "Conclusion"

I learned from my two years' experience that it would cost incredibly little trouble to obtain one's necessary food, even in this latitude; that a man may use as simple a diet as the animals, and yet retain health and strength. I have made a satisfactory dinner, satisfactory on several accounts, simply off a dish of purslane (*Portulaca oleracea*) which I gathered in my cornfield, boiled and salted. I give the Latin on account of the savoriness of the trivial name. And pray what more can a reasonable man desire, in peaceful times, in ordinary noons, than a sufficient number of ears of green sweet corn boiled, with the addition of salt?

Walden, "Economy"

IN ADAMS FALL

In Adams fall
We sinned all.
In the new Adam's rise.
We shall all reach the skies.

Great God, I ask thee for no meaner pelf
Than that I may not disappoint myself,
That in my action I may soar as high,
As I can now discern with this clear eye.

And next in value, which thy kindness lends,
That I may greatly disappoint my friends,
Howe'er they think or hope that it may be,
They may not dream how thou'st distinguished me.

That my weak hand may equal my firm faith,
And my life practice more than my tongue saith;
That my low conduct may not show,
Nor my relenting lines,
That I thy purpose did not know,
Or overrated thy designs.

The poet is he that hath fat enough, like bears and marmots, to suck his claws all winter. He hibernates in this world, and feeds on his own marrow. It is pleasant to think in winter, as we walk over the snowy pastures, of those happy dreamers that lie under the sod, of dormice and all that race of dormant creatures, which have such a superfluity of life enveloped in thick folds of fur, impervious to cold. Alas, the poet too is, in one sense, a sort of dormouse gone into winter quarters of deep and serene thoughts, insensible to surrounding circumstances, . . .

A Week on the Concord and Merrimack Rivers, "Sunday"

IN THE EAST FAMES ARE WON

In the East fames are won,
In the West deeds are done.

THE NEEDLES OF THE PINE

The needles of the pine,
All to the west incline.

The millions are awake enough for physical labor; but only one in a million is awake enough for effective intellectual exertion, only one in a hundred millions to a poetic or divine life. To be awake is to be alive. I have never yet met a man who was quite awake. How could I have looked him in the face?

Walden, "Where I Lived, and What I Lived For"

ON THE SUN COMING OUT IN THE AFTERNOON

Methinks all things have travelled since you shined,
But only Time, and clouds, Time's team, have moved;
Again foul weather shall not change my mind,
But in the shade I will believe what in the sun I loved.

from INSPIRATION

I hear beyond the range of sound,
   I see beyond the range of sight,
New earths and skies and seas around,
   And in my day the sun doth pale his light.

A clear and ancient harmony
   Pierces my soul through all its din,
As through its utmost melody,—
   Farther behind than they—farther within.

. . . . .

Such fragrance round my couch it makes,
   More rich than are Arabian drugs,
That my soul scents its life and wakes
   The body up beneath its perfumed rugs.

. . . . .

I will not doubt forever more,
   Nor falter from a steadfast faith,
For though the system be turned o'er,
   God takes not back the word which once he saith.

I will then trust the love untold
   Which not my worth nor want has bought,
Which wooed me young and woos me old,
   And to this evening hath me brought.

. . . . .

What's the railroad to me?
I never go to see
Where it ends.
It fills a few hollows,
And makes banks for the swallows,
It sets the sand a-blowing,
And the blackberries a-growing.

I walk in nature still alone
   And know no one
Discern no lineament nor feature
   Of any creature.

Though all the firmament
   Is o'er me bent,
Yet still I miss the grace
   Of an intelligent and kindred face.

I still must seek the friend
Who does with nature blend,
Who is the person in her mask,
He is the man I ask.

Who is the expression of her meaning,
Who is the uprightness of her leaning,
Who is the grown child of her weaning.

The center of this world,
The face of nature,
The site of human life,
Some sure foundation
And nucleus of a nation—
At least a private station.

We twain would walk together
Through every weather,
And see this aged nature,
Go with a bending stature.

I long ago lost a hound, a bay horse, and a turtledove, and am still on their trail. Many are the travellers I have spoken concerning them, describing their tracks and what calls they answered to. I have met one or two who had heard the hound, and the tramp of the horse, and even seen the dove disappear behind a cloud, and they seemed as anxious to recover them as if they had lost them themselves.

Walden, "Economy"

YOU MUST NOT ONLY AIM ARIGHT

You must not only aim aright,
But draw the bow with all your might.

There was an artist in the city of Kuoroo who was disposed to strive after perfection. One day it came into his mind to make a staff. Having considered that in an imperfect work time is an ingredient, but into a perfect work time does not enter, he said to himself, It shall be perfect in all respects, though I should do nothing else in my life. He proceeded instantly to the forest for wood, being resolved that it should not be made of unsuitable material; and as he searched for and rejected stick after stick, his friends gradually deserted him, for they grew old in their works and died, but he grew not older by a moment. His singleness of purpose and resolution, and his elevated piety, endowed him, without his knowledge, with perennial youth. As he made no compromise with Time, Time kept out of his way, and only sighed at a distance because he could not overcome him. Before he had found a stick in all respects suitable the city of Kuoroo was a hoary ruin, and he sat on one of its mounds to peel the stick. Before he had given it the proper shape the dynasty of the Candahars was at an end, and with the point of the stick he wrote the name of the last of that race in the sand, and then resumed his work. By the time he had smoothed and polished the staff Kalpa was no longer the pole-star; and ere he had put on the ferule and the head adorned with precious stones, Brahma had awoke and slumbered many times.

Walden, "Conclusion"

Among the worst of men that ever lived
However we did seriously attend
A little space we let our thoughts ascend
Experienced our religion & confessed
'Twas good for us to be there—be anywhere
Then to a heap of apples we addressed
& cleared the topmost rider *sine* care
But our Icarian thoughts returned to ground
And we went on to heaven the long way round.

PART FOUR

Seeing What Is Before Us

SEEING WHAT IS BEFORE US

T HOREAU WAS CAPABLE of true patience in observing the nonhuman world, and he exclaims in one passage, "Would it not be a luxury to stand up to one's chin in some retired swamp for a whole summer's day?" If we've read Thoreau, we know that he would be perfectly capable of it. He walked two to four hours each day and noted with the most astonishing perseverance and tenacity the exact days on which wildflowers—dozens of varieties—opened in the forest. In 1853 he notes in his journal: "My Aunt Maria asked me to read the life of Dr. Chalmers, which, however, I did not promise to do. Yesterday, Sunday, she was heard through the partition shouting to my Aunt Jane, who is deaf: 'Think of it: He stood half an hour today to hear the frogs croak, and he wouldn't read the life of Chalmers.'"

His neighbors saw him stand motionless for eight hours beside a pond to watch young frogs, and all day at a river's edge watching duck eggs hatching.

Thoreau felt invited to observe the detail in nature, and he did not receive this invitation from Wordsworth or Milton: it came to him as a part of his genius. When he was twenty-one he wrote in his journal: "Nature will bear the closest inspection. She invites us to lay our eye level with her smallest leaf, and take an insect view of its plain." There is something brilliant in the last clause, advising us to take a low-lying, or insect, position when we look. One day, while he lay on his back during a soaking rain, he saw a raindrop descend along a stalk of the previous year's oats. "While these clouds and this sombre drizzling weather shut all in, we two draw nearer and know one another," he wrote in his journal (March 30, 1840). R. H. Blyth declared this sentence to be one of the few sentences in the English language that was a genuine haiku.

Emerson said this of Thoreau's patience in his "Biographical Sketch":

It was a pleasure and a privilege to walk with him. He knew the country like a fox or a bird, and passed through it as freely by paths of his own. He knew every track in the snow or on the ground, and what creature had taken this path before him. One must submit abjectly to such a guide, and the reward was great. Under his arm he carried an old music-book to press plants; in his pocket, his diary and pencil, a spy-glass for birds, microscope, jack-knife, and twine. He wore a straw hat, stout shoes, strong gray trousers, to brave scrub-oaks and smilax, and to climb a tree for a hawk's or a squirrel's nest. He waded into the pool for the water-plants, and his strong legs were no insignificant part of his armor. On the day I speak of he looked for the Menyanthes, detected it across the wide pool, and, on examination of the florets, decided that it had been in flower five days. He drew out of his breast-pocket his diary, and read the names of all the plants that should bloom on this day, whereof he kept account as a banker when his notes fall due. The Cypripedium not due till to-morrow. He thought that, if waked up from a trance, in this swamp, he could tell by the plants what time of the year it was within two days. The redstart was flying about, and presently the fine grosbeaks, whose brilliant scarlet "makes the rash gazer wipe his eye," and whose fine clear note Thoreau compared to that of a tanager which has got rid of its hoarseness. . . .

. . . His power of observation seemed to indicate additional senses. He saw as with microscope, heard as with ear trumpet, and his memory was a photographic register of all he saw and heard.

We need to understand that Thoreau received through Emerson and Coleridge, through the Eastern spiritual books he read, among them those of the Indian poet Kabir, and through Goethe, Schelling and other German writers, the doctrine that the spiritual world lies hidden in, or moving among, or shining through the physical world. Nature is one of the languages that God speaks. He spoke in Hebrew—New Englanders had always known that—but the truth of the soul's interior abundance, while not denying that, added that He also spoke the local language called nature.

Since the physical world conceals or embodies a spiritual world, if one studies facts in nature, one might be able to deduce or distill from many physical facts a spiritual fact. Robert Frost, who is Thoreau's greatest disciple, hinted at that in his poem "Mowing":

There was never a sound beside the wood but one,
And that was my long scythe whispering to the ground.
What was it it whispered? I knew not well myself;
Perhaps it was something about the heat of the sun,
Something, perhaps, about the lack of sound—
And that was why it whispered and did not speak.
It was no dream of the gift of idle hours,
Or easy gold at the hand of fay or elf:
Anything more than the truth would have seemed too weak
To the earnest love that laid the swale in rows,
Not without feeble-pointed spikes of flowers
(Pale orchises), and scared a bright green snake.
The fact is the sweetest dream that labor knows.
My long scythe whispered and left the hay to make.

Thoreau remarked in his journal on February 18, 1852:

I have a commonplace book for facts, and another for poetry, but I find it difficult always to preserve the vague distinction which I had in mind, for the most interesting and beautiful facts are so much the more poetry and that is their success. They are translated from earth to heaven. I see that if my facts were sufficiently vital and significant—perhaps transmuted into the substance of the human mind—I should need but one book of poetry to contain them all.

So one can translate certain facts "from earth to heaven." Scientists, because they do not know Kabir's truth of the double world, do not translate. Scientific study of facts in Thoreau's time did not encourage the scientist to cross over the threshold between worlds. But Thoreau is able to cross from earth to heaven: "I see that if my facts were sufficiently vital and significant—perhaps transmuted into the substance of the human mind"—they would become poetry.

We understand that Thoreau's observation is not a simple-minded cataloging of detail. Behind his persistence lies the promise, grounded in his vast reading, that, in Coleridge's words, "each object rightly seen unlocks a new faculty of the Soul." What is it like, then, to look at an object rightly? Suppose one watched ants fighting. Eyes see surprises, polarities, nuances; the observer's language, if he or she wrote of the battle, would have to contain those nuances, so that the reader could also see rightly. We notice in the following passage that Thoreau provides "embraces," "sunny valley" and "chips" as nuances among the violence:

I watched a couple that were fast locked in each other's embraces, in a little sunny valley amid the chips, now at noonday prepared to fight till the sun went down, or life went out. The smaller red champion had fastened himself like a vice to his adversary's front, and through all the tumblings on that field never for an instant ceased to gnaw at one of his feelers near the root, having already caused the other to go by the board; while the stronger black one dashed him from side to side, and, as I saw on looking nearer, had already divested him of several of his members. They fought with more pertinacity than bulldogs.

How good "pertinacity" is here! The swift changes of mood in animal encounters, the intricacy of instinctual gesture, the mixture of comical and tragical, require a vocabulary that can go from high to low in an instant, that can move from dark to light and back, from metallic word to fragrant word, from a slang phrase to words from the Middle Ages or the eighteenth century. American democracy suggests that good writing about nature requires only a simple heart; but bravery of soul, immense learning and cunning in language—none of them simple—are what nature writing requires.

We recognize that Thoreau's account of the ant battle is not pure observation without human imposition; while he observes detail, he is also declaring that men's proclivity for battle is mechanical and antlike:

Holding a microscope to the first-mentioned red ant, I saw that, though he was assiduously gnawing at the near foreleg of his enemy, having severed his remaining feeler, his own breast was all torn away, exposing what vitals he had there to the jaws of the black warrior, whose breastplate was apparently too thick for him to pierce; and the dark carbuncles of the sufferer's eyes shone with ferocity such as war only could excite.

"Assiduously" is essential here. Long, "unnatural" words suggest the fierce intensity of the insect world, in which no one is "laid back" in the California way. Thoreau places "feeler," a word a child might use, near "vitals," an adult word that evokes complicated feelings, including fear. He mingles with that "black warrior" and "breastplate," words that carry a Middle Ages fragrance, and they prepare for the astonishing phrase "dark carbuncles of the sufferer's eyes."

Thoreau writes with equal cunning when he composes less tendentious description—for example, when he describes a squirrel chewing on successive ears of corn. His language then imposes fewer human analogies, becomes amazingly quick-footed, and his nimble rhythms seem transparent to the animal's consciousness.

Thoreau attempts something new in American literature. He does not agree with earlier New Englanders that the world is fallen, and a dark ruin, but believes by contrast that the world remains radiant from the divine energy that shines through it. A few days before he died, a family friend asked him "how he stood affected toward Christ." Thoreau answered, as reported in the *Christian Examiner* in 1865, that "a snow-storm was more to him than Christ." He is suggesting, I think, that even in the 1860s, so far into the nineteenth century, the snowstorm is still luminous with spiritual energy; and Christ is not needed to lift it back up into radiance. The snowstorm and God had never quarreled.

Thoreau trained himself over many years to see. His training involved a number of disciplines. The first was constant labor. His journals are so immense that they must have required, during his short life, two or three hours of writing each day, over and above the walks he wrote about. Second, he aimed to become just, and in this struggle followed the ancient doctrine, contrary to scientific doctrine, that certain secrets of nature reveal themselves only to the observer who is morally developed. The alchemists founded their penetration of nature on their moral character. Concentrating on a "low-anchored cloud," Thoreau wrote:

> *Drifting meadow of the air,*
> *Where bloom the daisied banks and violets,*
> *And in whose fenny labyrinth*
> *The bittern booms and heron wades;*
> *Spirit of lakes and seas and rivers,*
> *Bear only perfumes and the scent*
> *Of healing herbs to just men's fields!*

Third, he aimed to diminish the distance between subject and object, to heal the split that intellect in general, and Descartes in particular, opened between man and nature. When Descartes distinguished between "the thing that thinks" and "the thing that has space," he widened the split between human beings and nature. Melville expressed the terror of this gap in a marvelous metaphor given to Ishmael: "If you lean away from the mast," Ishmael says, "over Descartian vortices you hover." Thoreau aimed to heal the Cartesian gap by studying the idea that forms and colors are adapted to the human eye. We do not have, then, two things—an eye on the one side and an incomprehensible, strange, nonhuman object on the other—but rather we have a human eye as natural as and a part of the meadow and the island: "I am made to love the pond and the meadow, . . ." (*Journal*, November 21, 1850) Thoreau grasped that such interchange means that a human being cannot discover his own makeup solely by studying history, or investigating his dreams, or noticing his reaction to other human beings. On the contrary that person will never understand himself or herself until he or she has consciously loved the pond and the meadow.

Thoreau trained himself also to see the darkness of apparently light-filled things. When we see smoke rising from an isolated farmhouse, we idealize the life by the hearth. Thoreau trained himself to see the mortgage and "the idiot sitting by the fire." When he visited Cape Cod, he described a woman he saw there:

We saw one singularly masculine woman, however, in a house on this very plain, who did not look as if she was ever troubled with hysterics, or sympathized with those who were; or, per-chance, life itself was to her a hysteric fit,—a Nauset woman, of a hardness and coarseness such as no man ever possesses or suggests. It was enough to see the vertebrae and sinews of her neck, and her set jaws of iron, which would have bitten a board-nail in two in their ordinary action,— braced against the world, talking like a man-of-war's-man in petticoats, or as if shouting to you through a breaker; who looked as if it made her head ache to live; hard enough for any enormity. I looked upon her as one who had committed infanticide; who never had a brother, unless it were some wee thing that died in infancy,—for what need of him?—and whose father must have died before she was born. (Cape Cod)

But he is not satisfied with his ability to see. One of his most magnificent poems is "Smoke":

> Light-winged Smoke, Icarian bird,
> Melting thy pinions in thy upward flight,
> Lark without song, and messenger of dawn,
> Circling above the hamlets as thy nest;
> Or else, departing dream, and shadowy form
> Of midnight vision, gathering up thy skirts;
> By night star-veiling, and by day

Darkening the light and blotting out the sun;
Go thou my incense upward from this hearth,
And ask the gods to pardon this clear flame.

Thoreau realized that if he were to succeed in seeing truly, he himself would have to take in more darkness. He noticed that smoke's associations are with dream and midnight vision, and that smoke veils the stars at night and darkens the sun by day, and so he wrote:

Go thou my incense upward from this hearth,
And ask the gods to pardon this clear flame.

We feel in Thoreau's life the presence of a fierce and long-lived discipline, and one reward of that discipline was his grasp of the wildness in nature.

I live so much in my habitual thoughts, a routine of thought, that I forget there is any outside to the globe, and am surprised when I behold it as now,—yonder hills and river in the moonlight, the monsters. Yet it is salutary to deal with the surface of things. What are these rivers and hills, these hieroglyphics which my eyes behold? There is something invigorating in this air, which I am peculiarly sensible is a real wind, blowing from over the surface of a planet. I look out at my eyes, I come to my window, and I feel and breathe the fresh air. It is a fact equally glorious with the most inward experience. Why have we ever slandered the outward?

Journal, August 23, 1852

Yesterday and to-day the stronger winds of autumn have begun to blow, and the telegraph harp has sounded loudly. I heard it especially in the Deep Cut this afternoon, the tone varying with the tension of different parts of the wire. The sound proceeds from near the posts, where the vibration is apparently more rapid. I put my ear to one of the posts, and it seemed to me as if every pore of the wood was filled with music, labored with the strain,—as if every fibre was affected and being seasoned or timed, rearranged according to a new and more harmonious law. Every swell and change or inflection of tone pervaded and seemed to proceed from the wood, the divine tree or wood, as if its very substance was transmuted. What a recipe for preserving wood, perchance,—to keep it from rotting,—to fill its pores with music! . . . When no music proceeds from the wire, on applying my ear I hear the hum within the entrails of the wood,—the oracular tree acquiring, accumulating, the prophetic fury.

Journal, September 22, 1851

Scared up three blue herons in the little pond close by, quite near us. It was a grand sight to see them rise, so slow and stately, so long and limber, with an undulating motion from head to foot, undulating also their large wings, undulating in two directions, and looking warily about them. With this graceful, limber, undulating motion they arose, as if so they got under way, their two legs trailing parallel far behind like an earthy residuum to be left behind. They are large, like birds of Syrian lands, and seemed to oppress the earth, and hush the hillside to silence, as they winged their way over it, looking back towards us.

Journal, April 19, 1852

... a neat herd of cows approached, of unusually fair proportions and smooth, clean skins, evidently petted by their owner, who must have carefully selected them. One more confiding heifer, the fairest of the herd, did by degrees approach as if to take some morsel from our hands, while our hearts leaped to our mouths with expectation and delight. She by degrees drew near with her fair limbs progressive, making pretense of browsing; nearer and nearer, till there was wafted toward us the bovine fragrance,—cream of all the dairies that ever were or will be,—and then she raised her gentle muzzle toward us, and snuffed an honest recognition within hand's reach. I saw 't was possible for his herd to inspire with love the herdsman. She was as delicately featured as a hind. Her hide was mingled white and fawn-color, and on her muzzle's tip there was a white spot not bigger than a daisy, and on her side toward me the map of Asia plain to see.

Journal, September 1850

. . . I heard a singular rattling sound, somewhat like that of the sticks which boys play with their fingers, when, looking up, I observed a very slight and graceful hawk, like a nighthawk, alternately soaring like a ripple and tumbling a rod or two over and over, showing the under side of its wings, which gleamed like satin ribbon in the sun, or like the pearly inside of a shell. . . . It was the most ethereal flight I had ever witnessed. It did not simply flutter like a butterfly, nor soar like the larger hawks, but it sported with proud reliance in the fields of air; mounting again and again with its strange chuckle, it repeated its free and beautiful fall, turning over and over like a kite, and then recovering from its lofty tumbling, as if it had never set its foot on *terra firma*. It appeared to have no companion in the universe,— sporting there alone,—and to need none but the morning and the ether with which it played. It was not lonely, but made all the earth lonely beneath it.

Walden, "Spring"

. . . . .

Here while I lie beneath this walnut bough,
What care I for the Greeks or for Troy town,
If juster battles are enacted now
Between the ants upon this hummock's crown?

Bid Homer wait still I the issue learn,
If red or black the gods will favor most,
Or yonder Ajax will the phalanx turn,
Struggling to heave some rock against the host.

Tell Shakespeare to attend some leisure hour,
For now I've business with this drop of dew,
And see you not, the clouds prepare a shower,—
I'll meet him shortly when the sky is blue.

. . . . .

I was witness to events of a less peaceful character. One day when I went out to my wood-pile, or rather my pile of stumps, I observed two large ants, the one red, the other much larger, nearly half an inch long, and black, fiercely contending with one another. Having once got hold they never let go, but struggled and wrestled and rolled on the chips incessantly. Looking farther, I was surprised to find that the chips were covered with such combatants, that it was not a *duellum*, but a *bellum*, a war between two races of ants, the red always pitted against the black, and frequently two red ones to one black. The legions of these Myrmidons covered all the hills and vales in my wood-yard, and the ground was already strewn with the dead and dying, both red and black. It was the only battle which I have ever witnessed, the only battle-field I ever trod while the battle was raging; internecine war; the red republicans on the one hand, and the black imperialists on the other. On every side they were engaged in deadly combat, yet without any noise that I could hear, and human soldiers never fought so resolutely. I watched a couple that were fast locked in each other's embraces, in a little sunny valley amid the chips, now at noonday prepared to fight till the sun went down, or life went out. The smaller red champion had fastened himself like a vice to his adversary's front, and through all the tumblings on that field never for an instant ceased to gnaw at one of his feelers near the root, having already caused the other to go by the board; while the stronger black one dashed him from side to side, and, as I saw on looking nearer, had already divested him of several of his members. They fought with more pertinacity than bulldogs. Neither manifested the least disposition to retreat. It was evident that their battle-cry was "Conquer or die." In the meanwhile there came along a single red ant on the hillside of this valley, evidently full of excitement, who either had despatched his foe, or had not yet taken part in the battle; probably the latter, for he had lost none of his limbs; whose mother had charged him to return with his shield or upon it. Or perchance he was some Achilles, who had nourished his wrath apart, and had now come to avenge or rescue his Patroclus. He saw this unequal combat from afar,—for the blacks were nearly twice the size of the red,— he drew near with rapid pace till he stood on his guard within half an inch of the combatants; then, watching his opportunity, he sprang upon the black warrior, and commenced his operations near the root of his right fore leg, leaving the foe to select among his own members; and so there were three united for life, as if a new kind of attraction had been invented which put all other locks and cements to shame. I should not have wondered by this time to find that they had their respective musical bands stationed on some eminent chip, and playing their national airs the while, to excite the slow and cheer the dying combatants. I was myself excited somewhat even as if they had been men. The more you think of it, the less the difference. And certainly there is not the fight recorded in Concord history, at least, if in the history of America, that will bear a moment's comparison with this, whether for the numbers engaged in it, or for the patriotism and heroism displayed. For numbers and for carnage it was an Austerlitz or Dresden. Concord Fight! Two killed on the patriots' side, and Luther Blanchard wounded! Why here every ant was a Buttrick,—"Fire! for God's sake fire!"—and thousands shared the fate of Davis and Hosmer. There was not one hireling there. I have no doubt that it was a principle they fought for, as much as our ancestors, and not to avoid a three-penny tax on their tea; and the results of this battle will be as important and memorable to those whom it concerns as those of the battle of Bunker Hill, at least.

I took up the chip on which the three I have particularly described were struggling, carried [it] into my house, and placed it under a tumbler on my window-sill, in order to see the issue. Holding a microscope to the first-mentioned red ant, I saw that, though he was assiduously gnawing at the near fore leg of his enemy, having severed his remaining feeler, his own breast was all torn away, exposing what vitals he had there to the jaws of the black warrior, whose breastplate was apparently too thick for him to pierce; and the dark carbuncles of the sufferer's eyes shone with ferocity such as war only could excite. They struggled half an hour longer under the tumbler, and when I looked again the black soldier had severed the heads of his foes from their bodies, and the still living heads were hanging on either side of him like ghastly trophies at his saddle-bow, still apparently as firmly fastened as ever, and he was endeavoring with feeble struggles, being without feelers and with only the remnant of a leg, and I know not how many other wounds, to divest himself of them; which at length, after half an hour more, he accomplished. I raised the glass, and he went off over the window-sill in that crippled state.

Walden, "Brute Neighbors"

THEY WHO PREPARE MY EVENING MEAL BELOW

They who prepare my evening meal below
Carelessly hit the kettle as they go
With tongs or shovel,
And ringing round and round,
Out of this hovel
It makes an eastern temple by the sound.

At first I thought a cow-bell right at hand
Mid birches sounded o'er the open land,
Where I plucked flowers
Many years ago,
Spending midsummer hours
With such secure delight they hardly seemed to flow.

I'VE HEARD MY NEIGHBOR'S PUMP AT NIGHT

I've heard my neighbor's pump at night,
Long after Lyra sunk her light,
As if it were a natural sound,
And proper utterance of the ground—
Perchance some bittern in a fen—
Or else the squeak of a meadow hen.

The sluggish smoke curls up from some deep dell,
The stiffened air exploring in the dawn,
And making slow acquaintance with the day;
Delaying now upon its heavenward course,
In wreathed loiterings dallying with itself,
With as uncertain purpose and slow deed,
As its half-wakened master by the hearth,
Whose mind still slumbering and sluggish thoughts
Have not yet swept into the onward current
Of the new day;—and now it streams afar,
The while the chopper goes with step direct,
And mind intent to swing the early axe.
First in the dusky dawn he sends abroad
His early scout, his emissary, smoke,
The earliest, latest pilgrim from the roof,
To feel the frosty air, inform the day;
And while he crouches still beside the hearth,
Nor musters courage to unbar the door,
It has gone down the glen with the light wind,
And o'er the plain unfurled its venturous wreath,
Draped the tree tops, loitered upon the hill,
And warmed the pinions of the early bird;
And now, perchance, high in the crispy air,
Has caught sight of the day o'er the earth's edge,
And greets its master's eye at his low door,
As some refulgent cloud in the upper sky.

As I turned round the corner of Hubbard's Grove, saw a woodchuck, the first of the season, in the middle of the field. . . . I ran along the fence and cut him off, . . . he stopped, and I did the same; . . . I squatted down and surveyed him at my leisure. . . . The head between a squirrel and a bear, flat on the top and dark brown, and darker still or black on the tip of the nose. The whiskers black, two inches long. The ears very small and roundish, set far back and nearly buried in the fur. Black feet, with long and slender claws for digging. It appeared to tremble, or perchance shivered with cold. When I moved, it gritted its teeth quite loud, sometimes striking the under jaw against the other chatteringly, sometimes grinding one jaw on the other, yet as if more from instinct than anger. Whichever way I turned, that way it headed. I took a twig a foot long and touched its snout, at which it started forward and bit the stick, lessening the distance between us to two feet, and still it held all the ground it gained. I played with it tenderly awhile with the stick, trying to open its gritting jaws. Ever its long incisors, two above and two below, were presented. But I thought it would go to sleep if I stayed long enough. It did not sit upright as sometimes, but *standing* on its fore feet with its head down, *i.e.* half sitting, half standing. We sat looking at one another about half an hour, till we began to feel mesmeric influence. . . . I walked round him; he turned as fast and fronted me still. I sat down by his side within a foot. I talked to him *quasi* forest lingo, baby-talk, at any rate in a conciliatory tone, and thought that I had some influence on him. He gritted his teeth less. I chewed checkerberry leaves and presented them to his nose at last without a grit; though I saw that by so much gritting of the teeth he had worn them rapidly and they were covered with a fine white powder, which, if you measured it thus, would have made his anger terrible. He did not mind any noise I might make. With a little stick I lifted one of his paws to examine it, and held it up at pleasure. I turned him over to see what color he was beneath (darker or more purely brown), though he turned himself back again sooner than I could have wished. . . . I spoke kindly to him. I reached checkerberry leaves to his mouth. I stretched my hands over him, though he turned up his head and still gritted a little. I laid my hand on him, but immediately took it off again, instinct not being wholly overcome. If I had had a few fresh bean leaves, thus in advance of the season, I am sure I should have tamed him completely. . . . I finally had to leave him without seeing him move from the place.

Journal, April 16, 1852

95

Suddenly, looking down the river, I saw a fox some sixty rods off, making across to the hills on my left. As the snow lay five inches deep, he made but slow progress, but it was no impediment to me. So, yielding to the instinct of the chase, I tossed my head aloft and bounded away, snuffing the air like a fox-hound, and spurning the world and the Humane Society at each bound. It seemed the woods rang with the hunter's horn, and Diana and all the satyrs joined in the chase and cheered me on. Oympian and Elean youths were waving palms on the hills. In the meanwhile I gained rapidly on the fox; but he showed a remarkable presence of mind, for, instead of keeping up the face of the hill, which was steep and unwooded in that part, he kept along the slope in the direction of the forest, though he lost ground by it. Notwithstanding his fright, he took no step which was not beautiful. The course on his part was a series of most graceful curves. It was a sort of leopard canter, I should say, as if he were nowise impeded by the snow, but were husbanding his strength all the while. When he doubled I wheeled and cut him off, bounding with fresh vigor, and Antaeus-like, recovering my strength each time I touched the snow. Having got near enough for a fair view, just as he was slipping into the wood, I gracefully yielded him the palm. He ran as though there were not a bone in his back, occasionally dropping his muzzle to the snow for a rod or two, and then tossing his head aloft when satisfied of his course. When he came to a declivity he put his fore feet together and slid down it like a cat. He trod so softly that you could not have heard it from any nearness, and yet with such expression that it would not have been quite inaudible at any distance. So, hoping this experience would prove a useful lesson to him, I returned to the village by the highway of the river.

Journal, January 30, 1841

Usually the red squirrel (*Sciurus hudsonius*) waked me in the dawn, coursing over the roof and up and down the sides of the house, as if sent out of the woods for this purpose. In the course of the winter I threw out half a bushel of ears of sweet corn, which had not got ripe, on to the snow-crust by my door, and was amused by watching the motions of the various animals which were baited by it. In the twilight and the night the rabbits came regularly and made a hearty meal. All day long the red squirrels came and went, and afforded me much entertainment by their maneuvers. One would approach at first warily through the shrub oaks, running over the snow crust by fits and starts like a leaf blown by the wind, now a few paces this way, with wonderful speed and waste of energy, making inconceivable haste with his "trotters," as if it were for a wager, and now as many paces that way, but never getting on more than half a rod at a time; and then suddenly pausing with a ludicrous expression and a gratuitous somerset, as if all the eyes in the universe were fixed on him,—for all the motions of a squirrel, even in the most solitary recesses of the forest, imply spectators as much as those of a dancing girl,—wasting more time in delay and circumspection than would have sufficed to walk the whole distance,— I never saw one walk,—and then suddenly, before you could say Jack Robinson, he would be in the top of a young pitch pine, winding up his clock and chiding all imaginary spectators, soliloquizing and talking to all the universe at the same time, —for no reason that I could ever detect, or he himself was aware of, I suspect. At length he would reach the corn, and selecting a suitable ear, frisk about in the same uncertain trigonometrical way to the topmost stick of my wood-pile, before my window, where he looked me in the face, and there sit for hours, supplying himself with a new ear from time to time, nibbling at first voraciously and throwing the half-naked cobs about; till at length he grew more dainty still and played with his food, tasting only the inside of the kernel, and the ear, which was held balanced over the stick by one paw, slipped from his careless grasp and fell to the ground, when he would look over at it with a ludicrous expression of uncertainty, as if suspecting that it had life, with a mind not made up whether to get it again, or a new one, or be off; now thinking of corn, then listening to hear what was in the wind. So the little impudent fellow would waste many an ear in a forenoon; till at last, seizing some longer and plumper one, considerably bigger than himself, and skillfully balancing it, he would set out with it to the woods, like a tiger with a buffalo, by the same zigzag course and frequent pauses, scratching along with it as if it were too heavy for him and falling all the while, making its fall a diagonal between a perpendicular and horizontal, being determined to put it through at any rate;—a singularly frivolous and whimsical fellow;—and so he would get off with it to where he lived, perhaps carry it to the top of a pine tree forty or fifty rods distant, and I would afterwards find the cobs strewn about the woods in various directions.

Walden, "Winter Animals"

Where they once dug for money,
But never found any;
Where sometimes Martial Miles
Singly files,
And Elijah Wood,
I fear for no good:
No other man,
Save Elisha Dugan,—
O man of wild habits,
Partridges and rabbits,
Who hast no cares
Only to set snares,
Who liv'st all alone,
Close to the bone,
And where life is sweetest
Constantly eatest.
When the spring stirs my blood
With the instinct to travel,
I can get enough gravel
On the Old Marlborough Road.
Nobody repairs it,
For nobody wears it;
It is a living way,
As the Christians say.
Not many there be
Who enter therein,
Only the guests of the
Irishman Quin.
What is it, what is it,
But a direction out there,
And the bare possibility
Of going somewhere?

. . . . .
If with fancy unfurled
   You leave your abode,
You may go round the world
   By the Old Marlborough Road.

This afternoon, being on Fair Haven Hill, I heard the sound of a saw, and soon after from the Cliff saw two men sawing down a noble pine beneath, about forty rods off. I resolved to watch it till it fell, the last of a dozen or more which were left when the forest was cut and for fifteen years have waved in solitary majesty over the sprout-land. I saw them like beavers or insects gnawing at the trunk of this noble tree, the diminutive manikins with their cross-cut saw which could scarcely span it. It towered up a hundred feet as I afterward found by measurement, one of the tallest probably in the township and straight as an arrow, but slanting a little toward the hillside, its top seen against the frozen river and the hills of Conantum. I watch closely to see when it begins to move. Now the sawers stop, and with an axe open a little on the side toward which it leans, that it may break the faster. And now their saw goes again. Now surely it is going; it is inclined one quarter of the quadrant, and, breathless, I expect its crashing fall. But no, I was mistaken; it has not moved an inch; it stands at the same angle as at first. It is fifteen minutes yet to its fall. Still its branches wave in the wind, as if it were destined to stand for a century, and the wind soughs through its needles as of yore; it is still a forest tree, the most majestic tree that waves over Musketaquid. The silvery sheen of the sunlight is reflected from its needles; it still affords an inaccessible crotch for the squirrel's nest; not a lichen has forsaken its mast-like stem, its raking mast,—the hill is the hulk. Now, now's the moment! The manikins at its base are fleeing from their crime. They have dropped the guilty saw and axe. How slowly and majestically it starts! as if it were only swayed by a summer breeze, and would return without a sigh to its location in the air. And now it fans the hillside with its fall, and it lies down to its bed in the valley, from which it is never to rise, as softly as a feather, folding its green mantle about it like a warrior, as if, tired of standing, it embraced the earth with silent joy, returning its elements to the dust again. But hark! there you only saw, but did not hear. There now comes up a deafening crash to these rocks, advertising you that even trees do not die without a groan. It rushes to embrace the earth, and mingle its elements with the dust. And now all is still once more and forever, both to eye and ear.

Journal, December 30, 1851

Low-anchored cloud,
Newfoundland air,
Fountain-head and source of rivers,
Dew-cloth, dream drapery,
And napkin spread by fays;
Drifting meadow of the air,
Where bloom the daisied banks and violets,
And in whose fenny labyrinth
The bittern booms and heron wades;
Spirit of lakes and seas and rivers,
Bear only perfumes and the scent
Of healing herbs to just men's fields!

Few phenomena gave me more delight than to observe the form which thawing sand and clay assume in flowing down the sides of a deep cut on the railroad through which I passed on my way to the village, a phenomenon not very common on so large a scale, though the number of freshly exposed banks of the right material must have been greatly multiplied since railroads were invented. The material was sand of every degree of fineness and of various rich colors, commonly mixed with a little clay. When the frost comes out in the spring, and even in a thawing day in the winter, the sand begins to flow down the slopes like lava, sometimes bursting out through the snow and overflowing it where no sand was to be seen before. Innumerable little streams overlap and interlace one with another, exhibiting a sort of hybrid product, which obeys half way the law of currents, and half way that of vegetation. As it flows it takes the forms of sappy leaves or vines, making heaps of pulpy sprays a foot or more in depth, and resembling, as you look down on them, the laciniated, lobed, and imbricated thalluses of some lichens; or you are reminded of coral, of leopards' paws or birds' feet, or brains or lungs or bowels, and excrements of all kinds. It is a truly *grotesque* vegetation, whose forms and color we see imitated in bronze, a sort of architectural foliage more ancient and typical than acanthus, chicory, ivy, vine, or any vegetable leaves. . . .

The whole bank, which is from twenty to forty feet high, is sometimes overlaid with a mass of this kind of foliage, or sandy rupture, for a quarter of a mile on one or both sides, the produce of one spring day. What makes this sand foliage remarkable is its springing into existence thus suddenly. When I see on the one side the inert bank,—for the sun acts on one side first,—and on the other this luxuriant foliage, the creation of an hour, I am affected as if in a peculiar sense I stood in the laboratory of the Artist who made the world and me,—had come to where he was still at work, sporting on this bank, and with excess of energy strewing his fresh designs about. I feel as if I were nearer to the vitals of the globe, for this sandy overflow is something such as foliaceous mass as the vitals of the animal body. You find thus in the very sands an anticipation of the vegetable leaf. No wonder that the earth expresses itself outwardly in leaves, it so labors with the idea inwardly. The atoms have already learned this law, and are pregnant by it. The overhanging leaf sees here its prototype. *Internally*, whether in the globe or animal body, it is a moist thick *lobe*, a word especially applicable to the liver and lungs and the *leaves* of fat (λειβω, *labor*, *lapsus*, to flow or slip downward, a lapsing; λοβός, *globus*, lobe, globe; also lap, flap, and many other words); *externally*, a dry thin *leaf*, even as the *f* and *v* are a pressed and dried *b*. The radicals of lobe are *lb*, the soft mass of the *b* (single-lobed, or B, doubled-lobed), with the liquid *l* behind it pressing it forward. In globe, *glb*, the guttural *g* adds to the meaning the capacity of the throat. The feathers and wings of birds are still drier and thinner leaves. Thus, also, you pass from the lumpish grub in the earth to the airy and fluttering butterfly. The very globe continually transcends and translates itself, and becomes winged in its orbit. Even ice begins with delicate crystal leaves, as if it had flowed into moulds which the fronds of water-plants have impressed on the watery mirror. The whole tree itself is but one leaf, and rivers are still vaster leaves whose pulp is intervening earth, and towns and cities are the ova of insects in their axils. . . .

Thus it seemed that this one hillside illustrated the principle of all the operations of Nature. The Maker of this earth but patented a leaf. What Champollion will decipher this hieroglyphic for us, that we may turn over a new leaf at last? This phenomenon is more exhilarating to me than the luxuriance and fertility of vineyards. True, it is somewhat excrementitious in its character, and there is no end to the heaps of liver, lights, and bowels, as if the globe were turned wrong side outward; but this suggests that Nature has at least some bowels, and there again is mother of humanity. This is the frost coming out of the ground; this is Spring. It precedes the green and flowery spring, as mythology precedes regular poetry.

Walden, "Spring"

PART FIVE

In Wildness Is the Preservation
of the World

PART FIVE

IN WILDNESS IS THE PRESERVATION OF THE WORLD

PHOTOGRAPHS OF THOREAU give a sense of sedateness and sobriety, and they determine our usual view of him; but he also had a grand interior wildness. He remarks in *Walden*, "As I came home through the woods with my string of fish, trailing my pole, it being now quite dark, I caught a glimpse of a woodchuck stealing across my path, and felt a strange thrill of savage delight, and was strongly tempted to seize and devour him raw. . . ."

Rose Hawthorne, in her book *Memories of Hawthorne*, left a lovely description of Hawthorne, Thoreau and Emerson skating. Hawthorne "moved like a self-impelled Greek statue, stately and grave," and Emerson moved as if "too weary to hold himself erect, pitching head foremost, half lying on the air." Thoreau did "dithyrambic dances and Bacchic leaps on the ice." A visitor to the Thoreau house, whose memoir Thoreau's biographer, Walter Harding, found, remembers that one evening Thoreau ran down from his upstairs study and broke into a dance, "spinning airily around, displaying most remarkable lightness and agility, and finally springing over the center table, alighting like a feather on the other side. . . ."

Of the marsh hawk Thoreau said, "There is health in thy gray wing," and he reminded the reader that "in literature it is only the wild that attracts us." We require that all things be mysterious and unchartable, that land and sea be infinitely wild, unsurveyed and unfathomed by us because unfathomable. He associated "wild" with "willed," with what is not passive and indecisive. And he was sure that the civilized nations—Greece, Rome, England—have "been sustained by the primitive forests" that surrounded them, and that these same nations have died and will die when the forests end.

The Spanish poet Antonio Machado, so like Thoreau in many ways, wrote this sentence about his own poems in the introduction to his *Selected Poems*: "Many of the poems spring from . . . a simple love of nature that in me is far stronger than the love of art." Few writers would state this sentiment so baldly, and we would not expect it from writers who love and practice their craft as artists. When Machado, —who was, like Thoreau, a great artist,—says it, we listen.

Moreover, I think that few men or women, artists or not, love nature and its wildness. Many people understand the truth that nature is a deeper friend of the soul than society. But, just because a person knows and believes this truth doesn't mean that he or she will love nature. We tend to love what is like us: Chaucer found the seasons thrilling, but he loved the Wife of Bath; the Anglo-Saxon poets admired nature as a terrible master, but they loved men who earned fame and had a great civil helpfulness; Jane Austen liked the garden, but she loved the soul's ability to make distinctions in feeling; Milton, when walking with a woman he loved, forgot all time—"all seasons and all change, all please alike"—he liked the wildness of nature, but he loved the rebellious impulse in the human soul.

In 1857 Thoreau wrote in his journal: "How rarely a man's love for nature becomes a ruling principle with him, like a youth's affection for a maiden, but more enduring: All nature is my bride." Five months earlier he had realized that he was about to become a husband: "There was a match found for me at last. I fell in love with a shrub oak."

On December 12, 1851, he also wrote in his journal: "Ah, dear nature, the mere remembrance, after a short forgetfulness, of the pine woods! I come to it as a hungry man to a crust of bread."

> *For I had rather be thy child*
> *And pupil in the forest wild*
> *Than be the king of men elsewhere*
> *And most sovereign slave of care,*
> *To have one moment of thy dawn*
> *Than share the city's year forlorn.*
> *Some still work give me to do*
> *Only be it near to you.*

We know the speculation that Thoreau loved nature because he couldn't love a woman, and I'll talk of that a little in the biographical sketch. But his love of nature, to me, is not to be reduced to something else: "I am made to love the pond and the meadow, as the wind is made to ripple the water."

Moreover, if nature is a woman he loves, who is his bride, we see that he is not loving a coarse, mechanistic, dull-headed woman, but rather a woman like Emerson's Aunt Mary, full of intelligence in every cell of her body. I have suggested that Thoreau was one of the first writers in America to accept the ancient idea that nature is not a fallen world, but on the contrary a veil for the divine world, the chest in which God is hidden, an alphabet whose vowels are a beam going straight to the kingdom of light, so that the owl's dark eyelids cover a luminosity our reason cannot grasp, let alone reason about.

If we use Blake's terms, the body of Thoreau's bride "is a portion of Soul discern'd by the five Senses, the chief inlets of Soul in this age," and each part of nature is holy. Blake says in "Auguries of Innocence":

> *A Robin Red breast in a Cage*
> *Puts all Heaven in a Rage.*

Thoreau, like Blake, was training himself to see *through*, not *with*, the eye. When people see only with the practical eye, they will see material beings, objects without light around them, pieces of inert nature, dead rocks, trees no more alive than the gears in a watch. Blake called such vision "single vision," and he said:

> *. . . May God us keep*
> *From single vision & Newton's sleep!*

The contrary way of seeing—seeing through the eye, or through the inner eye—leads us to glimpse the divine energy in each thing we see:

> *To see a World in a Grain of Sand*
> *And a Heaven in a Wild Flower,*
> *Hold Infinity in the palm of your hand,*
> *And Eternity in an hour.*

> "Auguries of Innocence"

As we read Thoreau's work, especially his prose, we slowly become aware of a light in and around the squirrel, the ant, the woodchuck, the hawk, that belongs to *them* and not to the eyes observing or the brain producing words. The human mind, when it is in its own deeps, shares that light, so that it is not always improper to bring in human feelings when describing an animal or object. When people insist on keeping all human feelings out, they mean to retain single vision.

Blake said:

> *For double the vision my Eyes do see,*
> *And a double vision is always with me.*
> *With my inward Eye 'tis an old Man grey;*
> *With my outward a Thistle across the Way.*

It isn't that Blake doesn't see the thistle; he sees the thistle with the eye, and then through the eye he sees in the thistle an old man gray. Thoreau does not aim to glimpse imaginary or fantasy figures while ignoring the physical world; on the contrary, he sees with the material eye marvelously; no detail escapes his attention. As Emerson remarked, "His power of observation seemed to indicate additional senses." But he wants to go further.

His journal entry of October 29, 1857, is a good example of his increasing respect for impalpable seeing. A recurrent dream came to Thoreau, and he wrote of it at last in this entry, roughly four-and-a-half years before he died. He saw in his dream a mountain near Concord that did not exist. He "steadily ascended along a rocky ridge half clad with stinted trees, where wild beasts haunted." He did not climb to a European or Christian Mount of Purgatory, but rather arrived at an American rocky mountain plateau, "bare and pathless rock." This bare and rocky peak participates in what the late-eighteenth-century poets called Terror, and which they contrasted to beneficent nature, or Beauty. "You know no path, but wander, thrilled, over the bare and pathless rock," Thoreau wrote. "In dreams I am shown this height from time to time." He added that walking on it resembles walking on the face of a god.

Two strange features of the dream strike him. First, the ascent begins where the "Burying Hill" is in ordinary life. "You might go through its gate to enter that dark wood, but that hill and its graves are so concealed and obliterated by the awful mountain that I never thought of them as underlying it." So one goes through the place of the dead to arrive at the wildness and the terror. The dead seem to be a part of that darkness that he, despite his efforts to approach it, had avoided too much in his life. The mountaintop participates in the terror that Goya and others had seen in nature, while he and Wordsworth, to name a writer akin to Thoreau, had seen primarily the beauty and order of nature.

Second, in his dreams he descended the mountain by going through a sunny pasture. That was strange, because he had never ascended that way. "There are ever two ways up: one is through the dark wood, the other through the sunny pasture." His psyche seems to be telling him that a whole new way of writing lies ahead of him. Descending the mountain in his dream, he entered the ordinary world through a sunny pasture, as Odysseus entered his old life in Ithaca through the gladsome swineherd's hut. Thoreau can now see the possibility of climbing the terror through a sunny pasture. He had often begun his books and poems with an image of imprisonment and ended them with an image of light. *Walden* ends with the statement "The sun is but a morning star." He was about to die of tuberculosis, yet the psyche, as Jung reported from the experience of many dying patients, seems to pay no attention to the impending death. The dream says, "You could write something wholly new now, beginning your ascent the other way." But Thoreau didn't live long enough to write this new sort of poem.

It only remains to say a few words about the qualities I love in Thoreau. I love his fierce and meticulous observation. Most artists begin, as seems right, with interior absorption, introversion and examination of their inner world, and often end there. From much ancient art, we deduce that the next stage involves attention, which goes to the life beyond one's house, beyond one's mind, beyond human obsession to the enormous intertangling that we call the universe. Thoreau got to this second stage, a place reached by very few artists of the last century.

I also love the density Thoreau developed in his own personality. He got rid of the collective expectations projected on him, as the community projects on us all, and filled those spaces with more Thoreau—more likes, opinions and original nature. He was named David Henry Thoreau, but he changed that, and became Henry David Thoreau everywhere in his body, and even in his dense and magnificent sentences. When he was an adult, he was not the sort of tree one cuts down to make a house. Even his old enemy, Daniel Shattuck, president of the local bank, said of him after he died, "Mr. Thoreau was a man who never conformed his opinions after the model of others; they were his own; were also singular. Who will say they were not right? He had many admirers, and well he might for, whatever might be the truth of his opinions, his life was one of singular purity and kindness." An ancient tree, hundreds of years old, once spoke to a Taoist who walked past it, and explained that it had got to its height, with its gnarled branches and bitter bark, by "being useless." Thoreau chose the way of bitter bark and gnarled branches and no one cut him down for a house.

Lastly, I love his genius at metaphorical thinking. All mythological thinking, as Joseph Campbell has so often stated, is metaphorical, and difficult to us for that reason. Thoreau noticed that an insect egg got caught inside an apple-wood table and hatched years after its secretion. Such a physical fact, when seen metaphorically, carries the observer into the soul or the inner world or the invisible world. Thoreau did not throw away the fact of the insect egg and its slow hatching, but loved it as a fact, until it carried him to the soul. He was a master of metaphorical thinking. In "The American Scholar," Emerson hoped that for his generation the ancient precept "Know thyself" and the contemporary precept "Study nature" would become a single precept, a single piece of advice, a single guide. In Thoreau the two joined.

In literature it is only the wild that attracts us. Dullness is but another name for tameness. It is the uncivilized free and wild thinking in Hamlet and the Iliad, in all the scriptures and mythologies, not learned in the schools, that delights us. As the wild duck is more swift and beautiful than the tame, so is the wild—the mallard—thought, which 'mid falling dews wings its way above the fens. A truly good book is something as natural, and as unexpectedly and unaccountably fair and perfect, as a wild-flower discovered on the prairies of the West or in the jungles of the East. Genius is a light which makes the darkness visible, like the lightning's flash, which perchance shatters the temple of knowledge itself,—and not a taper lighted at the hearth-stone of the race, which pales before the light of common day.

"Walking"

I love and could embrace the shrub oak with its scanty garment of leaves rising above the snow, lowly whispering to me, akin to winter thoughts, and sunsets, and to all virtue. Covert which the hare and the partridge seek, and I too seek. What cousin of mine is the shrub oak? How can any man suffer long? For a sense of want is a prayer, and all prayers are answered. Rigid as iron, clean as the atmosphere, hardy as virtue, innocent and sweet as a maiden is the shrub oak. In proportion as I know and love it, I am natural and sound as a partridge.

Journal, December 1, 1856

Dull water spirit—and Protean god
Descended cloud fast anchored to the earth
That drawest too much air for shallow coasts
Thou ocean branch that flowest to the sun
Incense of earth, perfumed with flowers—
Spirit of lakes and rivers, seas and rills
Come to revisit now thy native scenes
Night thoughts of earth—dream drapery
Dew cloth and fairy napkin
Thou wind-blown meadow of the air.

Our village life would stagnate if it were not for the unexplored forests and meadows which surround it. We need the tonic of wildness,—to wade sometimes in marshes where the bittern and the meadow-hen lurk, and hear the booming of the snipe; to smell the whispering sedge where only some wilder and more solitary fowl builds her nest, and the mink crawls with its belly close to the ground. At the same time that we are earnest to explore and learn all things, we require that all things be mysterious and unexplorable, that land and sea be infinitely wild, unsurveyed and unfathomed by us because unfathomable. We can never have enough of nature. We must be refreshed by the sight of inexhaustible vigor, vast and titanic features, the sea-coast with its wrecks, the wilderness with its living and its decaying trees, the thunder-cloud, and the rain which lasts three weeks and produces freshets. We need to witness our own limits transgressed, and some life pasturing freely where we never wander. We are cheered when we observe the vulture feeding on the carrion which disgusts and disheartens us, and deriving health and strength from the repast. There was a dead horse in the hollow by the path to my house, which compelled me sometimes to go out of my way, especially in the night when the air was heavy, but the assurance it gave me of the strong appetite and inviolable health of Nature was my compensation for this. I love to see that Nature is so rife with life that myriads can be afforded to be sacrificed and suffered to prey on one another; that tender organizations can be so serenely squashed out of existence like pulp,—tadpoles which herons gobble up, and tortoises and toads run over in the road; and that sometimes it has rained flesh and blood! With the liability to accident, we must see how little account is to be made of it. The impression made on a wise man is that of universal innocence.

Walden, "Spring"

116

The hen-hawk and the pine are friends. The same thing which keeps the hen-hawk in the woods, away from the cities, keeps me here. That bird settles with confidence on a white pine top and not upon your weathercock. That bird will not be poultry of yours, lays no eggs for you, forever hides its nest. Though willed, or *wild*, it is not willful in its wildness. The unsympathizing man regards the wildness of some animals, their strangeness to him, as a sin; as if all their virtue consisted in their tamableness. He has always a charge in his gun ready for their extermination. What we call wildness is a civilization other than our own. The hen-hawk shuns the farmer, but it seeks the friendly shelter and support of the pine. It will not consent to walk in the barn-yard, but it loves to soar above the clouds. It has its own way and is beautiful, when we would fain subject it to our will. So any surpassing work of art is strange and wild to the mass of men, as is genius itself. No hawk that soars and steals our poultry is wilder than genius, and none is more persecuted or above persecution. It can never be poet laureate, to say "Pretty Poll" and "Polly want a cracker."

Journal, February 16, 1859

To preserve wild animals implies generally the creation of a forest for them to dwell in or resort to. So it is with man. . . .

The civilized nations—Greece, Rome, England—have been sustained by the primitive forests which anciently rotted where they stand. They survive as long as the soil is not exhausted. Alas for human culture! little is to be expected of a nation, when the vegetable mould is exhausted, and it is compelled to make manure of the bones of its fathers.

"Walking"

THE ROSA SANGUINEA

As often as a martyr dies,
This opes its petals to the skies;
And Nature by this trace alone
Informs us which way he is gone.

I have never felt lonesome, or in the least oppressed by a sense of solitude, but once, and that was a few weeks after I came to the woods, when, for an hour, I doubted if the near neighborhood of man was not essential to a serene and healthy life. To be alone was something unpleasant. But I was at the same time conscious of a slight insanity in my mood, and seemed to foresee my recovery. In the midst of a gentle rain while these thoughts prevailed, I was suddenly sensible of such sweet and beneficent society in Nature, in the very patterning of the drops, and in every sound and sight around my house, an infinite and unaccountable friendliness all at once like an atmosphere sustaining me, as made the fancied advantages of human neighborhood insignificant, and I have never thought of them since. Every little pine needle expanded and swelled with sympathy and befriended me. I was so distinctly made aware of the presence of something kindred to me, even in scenes which we are accustomed to call wild and dreary, and also that the nearest of blood to me and humanest was not a person or a villager, that I thought no place could ever be strange to me again.

Walden, "Solitude"

I was also serenaded by a hooting owl. Near at hand you could fancy it the most melancholy sound in Nature, as if she meant by this to stereotype and make permanent in her choir the dying moans of a human being,—some poor weak relic of mortality who has left hope behind, and howls like an animal, yet with human sobs, on entering the dark valley, made more awful by a certain gurgling melodiousness,—I find myself beginning with the letters *gl* when I try to imitate it,—expressive of a mind which has reached the gelationous, mildewy stage in the mortification of all healthy and courageous thought. It reminded me of ghouls and idiots and insane howlings. But now one answers from far woods in a strain made really melodious by distance,—*Hoo hoo hoo, hoorer hoo*; and indeed for the most part it suggested only pleasing associations, whether heard by day or night, summer or winter.

I rejoice that there are owls. Let them do the idiotic and maniacal hooting for men. It is a sound admirably suited to swamps and twilight woods which no day illustrates, suggesting a vast and undeveloped nature which men have not recognized. They represent the stark twilight and unsatisfied thoughts which all have. All day the sun has shone on the surface of some savage swamp, where the single spruce stands hung with usnea lichens, and small hawks circulate above, and the chickadee lisps amid the evergreens, and the partridge and rabbit skulk beneath; but now a more dismal and fitting day dawns, and a different race of creatures awakes to express the meaning of Nature there.

Walden, "Sounds"

SMOKE

Light-winged Smoke, Icarian bird,
Melting thy pinions in thy upward flight,
Lark without song, and messenger of dawn,
Circling above the hamlets as thy nest;
Or else, departing dream, and shadowy form
Of midnight vision, gathering up thy skirts;
By night star-veiling, and by day
Darkening the light and blotting out the sun;
Go thou my incense upward from this hearth,
And ask the gods to pardon this clear flame.

I saw Fair Haven Pond with its island, and meadow between the island and the shore, and a strip of perfectly still and smooth water in the lee of the island, and two hawks, fish hawks perhaps, sailing over it. I did not see how it could be improved. Yet I do not see what these things can be. I begin to see such an object when I cease to *understand* it and see that I did not realize or appreciate it before, but I get no further than this. How adapted these forms and colors to my eye! A meadow and an island! What are these things? Yet the hawks and the ducks keep so aloof! and Nature so reserved! I am made to love the pond and the meadow, as the wind is made to ripple the water.

Journal, November 21, 1850

The West of which I speak is but another name for the Wild; and what I have been preparing to say is, that in Wildness is the preservation of the World. . . . It was because the children of the Empire were not suckled by the wolf that they were conquered and displaced by the children of the northern forests who were.

I believe in the forest, and in the meadow, and in the night in which the corn grows.

"Walking"

As I came home through the woods with my string of fish, trailing my pole, it being now quite dark, I caught a glimpse of a woodchuck stealing across my path, and felt a strange thrill of savage delight, and was strongly tempted to seize and devour him raw; not that I was hungry then, except for that wildness which he represented. Once or twice, however, while I lived at the pond, I found myself ranging the woods, like a half-starved hound, with a strange abandonment, seeking some kind of venison which I might devour, and no morsel could have been too savage for me.

Walden, "Higher Laws"

TO A MARSH HAWK IN SPRING

There is health in thy gray wing
Health of nature's furnishing.
Say thou modern-winged antique,
Was thy mistress ever sick?
In each heaving of thy wing
Thou dost health and leisure bring,
Thou dost waive disease & pain
And resume new life again.

GREATER IS THE DEPTH OF SADNESS

Greater is the depth of sadness
Than is any height of gladness.

Every morning was a cheerful invitation to make my life of equal simplicity, and I may say innocence, with Nature herself. I have been as sincere a worshipper of Aurora as the Greeks. I got up early and bathed in the pond; that was a religious exercise, and one of the best things which I did. They say that characters were engraven on the bathing tub of King Tching-thang to this effect: "Renew thyself completely each day; do it again, and again, and forever again." I can understand that. Morning brings back the heroic ages. I was as much affected by the faint hum of a mosquito making its invisible and unimaginable tour through my apartment at earliest dawn, when I was sitting with door and windows open, as I could be by any trumpet that ever sang of fame. It was Homer's requiem; itself an Iliad and Odyssey in the air, singing its own wrath and wanderings. There was something cosmical about it; a standing advertisement, till forbidden, of the everlasting vigor and fertility of the world.

Walden, "Where I Lived, and What I Lived For"

The day has gone by with its wind like the wind of a cannonball, and now far in the west it blows. By that dun-colored sky you may track it. There is no motion nor sound in the woods (Hubbard's Grove) along which I am walking. The trees stand like great screens against the sky. The distant village sounds are the barking of dogs, that animal with which man has allied himself, and the rattling of wagons, for the farmers have gone into town a-shopping this Saturday night. The dog is the tamed wolf, as the villager is the tamed savage. But near, the crickets are heard in the grass, chirping from everlasting to everlasting, a mosquito sings near my ear, and the humming of a dor-bug drowns all the noise of the village, so roomy is the universe. The moon comes out of the mackerel cloud, and the traveller rejoices. How can a man write the same thoughts by the light of the moon, resting his book on a rail by the side of a remote potato-field, that he does by the light of the sun, on his study table? The light is but a luminousness. My pencil seems to move through a creamy, mystic medium. The moonlight is rich and somewhat opaque, like cream, but the daylight is thin and blue, like skimmed milk. I am less conscious than in the presence of the sun; my instincts have more influence.

Journal, June 18, 1853

When in some cove I lie,
A placid lake at rest,
Scanning the distant hills,
A murmur from the west,
And gleam of thousand rills
Which gently swell my breast,
Announce the friendly thought,
And in one wave sun-lit
I'm softly brought
Seaward with it.

Within the circuit of this plodding life
There enter moments of an azure hue,
Untarnished fair as is the violet
Or anemone, when the spring strews them
By some meandering rivulet, which make
The best philosophy untrue that aims
But to console man for his grievances.
I have remembered when the winter came,
High in my chamber in the frosty nights,
When in the still light of the cheerful moon,
On every twig and rail and jutting spout,
The icy spears were adding to their length
Against the arrows of the coming sun,
How in the shimmering noon of summer past
Some unrecorded beam slanted across
The upland pastures where the Johnswort grew;
Or heard, amid the verdure of my mind,
The bee's long smothered hum, on the blue flag
Loitering amidst the mead; or busy rill,
Which now through all its course stands still and dumb
Its own memorial,—purling at its play
Along the slopes, and through the meadows next,
Until its youthful sound was hushed at last
In the staid current of the lowland stream;
Or seen the furrows shine but late upturned,
And where the fieldfare followed in the rear,
When all the fields around lay bound and hoar
Beneath a thick integument of snow.
So by God's cheap economy made rich
To go upon my winter's task again.

I have occasional visits in the long winter evenings, when the snow falls fast and the wind howls in the wood, from an old settler and original proprietor, who is reported to have dug Walden Pond, and stoned it, and fringed it with pine woods; who tells me stories of old time and of new eternity; and between us we manage to pass a cheerful evening with social mirth and pleasant views of things, even without apples or cider,—a most wise and humorous friend, whom I love much, who keeps himself more secret than ever did Goffe or Whalley; and though he is thought to be dead, none can show where he is buried. An elderly dame, too, dwells in my neighborhood, invisible to most persons, in whose odorous herb garden I love to stroll sometimes, gathering simples and listening to her fables; for she has a genius of unequalled fertility, and her memory runs back farther than mythology, and she can tell me the original of every fable, and on what fact every one is founded, for the incidents occurred when she was young. A ruddy and lusty old dame, who delights in all weathers and seasons, and is likely to outlive all her children yet.

Walden, "Solitude"

This is a delicious evening, when the whole body is one sense, and imbibes delight through every pore. I go and come with a strange liberty in Nature, a part of herself. As I walk along the stony shore of the pond in my shirt-sleeves, though it is cool as well as cloudy and windy, and I see nothing special to attract me, all the elements are unusually congenial to me. The bullfrogs trump to usher in the night, and the note of the whip-poor-will is borne on the rippling wind from over the water. Sympathy with the fluttering alder and poplar leaves almost takes away my breath; yet, like the lake, my serenity is rippled but not ruffled.

Walden, "Solitude"

Woof of the sun, ethereal gauze,
Woven of Nature's richest stuffs,
Visible heat, air-water, and dry sea,
Last conquest of the eye;
Toil of the day displayed, sun-dust,
Aerial surf upon the shores of earth,
Ethereal estuary, frith of light,
Breakers of air, billows of heat,
Fine summer spray on inland seas;
Bird of the sun, transparent-winged
Owlet of noon, soft-pinioned,
From heath or stubble rising without song;
Establish thy serenity o'er the fields.

How different the ramrod jingle of the chewink or any bird's note sounds now at 5 P.M. in the cooler, stiller air, when also the humming of insects is more distinctly heard, and perchance some impurity has begun to sink to earth strained by the air! Or is it, perchance, to be referred to the cooler, more clarified and pensive state of the mind, when dews have begun to descend in it and clarify it? Chaste eve! A certain lateness in the sound, pleasing to hear, which releases me from the obligation to return in any particular season. I have passed the Rubicon of staying out. I have said to myself, that way is not homeward; I will wander further from what I have called my home—to the home which is forever inviting me. In such an hour the freedom of the woods is offered me, and the birds sing my dispensation. In dreams the links of life are united: we forget that our friends are dead; we know them as of old.

Journal, May 23, 1853

Men say they know many things;
But lo! they have taken wings,—
The arts and sciences,
And a thousand appliances;
The wind that blows
Is all that any body knows.

EACH SUMMER SOUND

Each summer sound
Is a summer round.

There are some things of which I cannot at once tell whether I have dreamed them or they are real; as if they were just, perchance, establishing, or else losing, a real basis in my world. This is especially the case in the early morning hours, when there is a gradual transition from dreams to waking thoughts, from illusions to actualities, as from darkness, or perchance moon and star light, to sunlight. Dreams are real, as is the light of the stars and moon, and theirs is said to be a *dreamy* light. Such early morning thoughts as I speak of occupy a debatable ground between dreams and waking thoughts. They are a sort of permanent dream in my mind. At least, until we have for some time changed our position from prostrate to erect, and commenced or faced some of the duties of the day, we cannot tell what we have dreamed from what we have actually experienced.

This morning, for instance, for the twentieth time at least, I thought of that mountain in the easterly part of our town (where no high hill actually is) which once or twice I had ascended, and often allowed my thoughts alone to climb. I now contemplate it in my mind as a familiar thought which I have surely had for many years from time to time, but whether anything could have reminded me of it in the middle of yesterday, whether I ever before remembered it in broad daylight, I doubt. I can now eke out the vision I had of it this morning with my old and yesterday forgotten dreams.

My way up used to lie through a dark and unfrequented wood at its base,—I cannot now tell exactly, it was so long ago, under what circumstances I first ascended, only that I shuddered as I went along (I have an indistinct remembrance of having been out overnight alone),—and then I steadily ascended along a rocky ridge half clad with stinted trees, where wild beasts haunted, till I lost myself quite in the upper air and clouds, seeming to pass an imaginary line which separates a hill, mere earth heaped up, from a mountain, into a superterranean grandeur and sublimity. What distinguishes that summit above the earthy line, is that it is unhandselled, awful, grand. It can never become familiar; you are lost the moment you set foot there. You know no path, but wander, thrilled, over the bare and pathless rock, as if it were solidified air and cloud. That rocky, misty summit, secreted in the clouds, was far more thrillingly awful and sublime than the crater of a volcano spouting fire.

This is a business we can partly understand. The perfect mountain height is already thoroughly purified. It is as if you trod with awe the face of a god turned up, unwittingly but helplessly, yielding to the laws of gravity. And are there not such mountains, east or west, from which you may look down on Concord in your thought, and on all the world? In dreams I am shown this height from time to time, and I seem to have asked my fellow once to climb there with me, and yet I am constrained to believe that I never actually ascended it. It chances, now I think of it, that it rises in my mind where lies the Burying Hill. You might go through its gate to enter that dark wood, but that hill and its graves are so concealed and obliterated by the awful mountain that I never thought of them as underlying it. Might not the graveyards of the just always be hills, ways by which we ascend and overlook the plain?

But my old way down was different, and, indeed, this was another way up, though I never so ascended. I came out, as I descended, breathing the thicker air. I came out the belt of wood into a familiar pasture, and along down by a wall. Often, as I go along the low side of this pasture, I let my thoughts ascend toward the mount, gradually entering the stinted wood (Nature subdued) and the thinner air, and drape themselves with mists. There are ever two ways up: one is through the dark wood, the other through the sunny pasture. That is, I reach and discover the mountain only through the dark wood, but I see to my surprise, when I look off between the mists from its summit, how it is ever adjacent to my native fields, nay, imminent over them, and accessible through a sunny pasture. Why is it that in the lives of men we hear more of the dark wood than of the sunny pasture?

A hard-featured god reposing, whose breath hangs about his forehead.

Journal, October 29, 1857

Now I go by the spring, and when I have risen to the same level as before, find myself in the warm stratum again.

The woods are about as destitute of inhabitants at night as the streets. In both there will be some night-walkers. . . .

The very cows have now left their pastures and are driven home to their yards. I meet no creature in the fields.

I hear the night-warbler breaking out as in his dreams, made so from the first for some mysterious reason.

Our spiritual side takes a more distinct form, like our shadow which we see accompanying us.

Journal, June 11, 1851

NATURE

O nature I do not aspire
To be the highest in thy quire,
To be a meteor in the sky
Or comet that may range on high,
Only a zephr that may blow
Among the reeds by the river low.
Give me thy most privy place
Where to run my airy race.
In some withdrawn unpublic mead
Let me sigh upon a reed,
Or in the woods with leafy din
Whisper the still evening in,
For I had rather be thy child
And pupil in the forest wild
Than be the king of men elsewhere
And most sovereign slave of care
To have one moment of thy dawn
Than share the city's year forlorn.
Some still work give me to do
Only be it near to you.

Henry David Thoreau was born, and given the name David Henry Thoreau, on July 12, 1817, in Concord, Massachusetts. His father's family went back to French Protestants who had moved to the Isle of Jersey after the Edict of Nantes in 1685; Henry's grandfather, John Thoreau, shipwrecked from a Jersey privateer, settled in Boston and alternated after that between business on land and attacking English ships at sea. Thoreau's father, John, was one of ten children. His mother's side of the family was lively and given to self-confident actions. Cynthia Thoreau's father, Asa Dunbar, led a rebellion when at Harvard against some inadequacy and became successively a schoolteacher, preacher and lawyer. Her mother, Mary Jones Dunbar, born to a line of Tories and slave owners, supported her Tory brothers when they were in prison during the Revolutionary War, slipped files to them in jail and helped them escape to Canada.

In the household into which Henry was born, Cynthia Thoreau struck all visitors as dominant. She was talkative, hard-working and a sharp-tongued reformer. Henry's father, John, opened several shops early in his life, but hesitated to collect debts. Eventually he succeeded in establishing a pencil-making factory. He was a flute player and lover of reading, and both Cynthia and John loved to walk in the woods and fields.

They had four children: Helen, John, Henry and Sophia. Henry was chosen to go to Harvard, though John seemed the more promising. Henry went, but never was enthusiastic about it, and did not rank very high in his class of fifty students. When he graduated in 1837 he walked home rather than stay for the ceremony. Later, when he asked his mother what he should do, she remarked that he could strap on his backpack and go out into the world. His sister Helen noticed that tears sprang to his eyes, and she put her arms around him and said, "No, Henry, you shall not go; you shall stay at home and live with us."

For the most part, that is exactly what he did. He lived for a time in other houses, but invariably returned. Neither of his two sisters married, and maiden aunts also lived in the house. He got a job teaching school, but abruptly resigned when he was required to flog a student. John and Henry later started a local school of their own, which lasted three years, closing at last in April of 1841 because of John's tuberculosis. During those years, both John and Henry fell in love with the same woman, Ellen Sewall, who was from Scituate, and Henry waited until John had proposed and been refused before he proposed. Ellen was a father's girl, and her father considered the Thoreau boys too advanced, being aware there was a transcendental taint to their thoughts. Ellen refused Henry as well. Shortly before he died, when his sister mentioned Ellen, Henry said, "I have always loved her. I have always loved her." It is possible that the turtledove he mentions losing in *Walden* was Ellen Sewall. On New Year's Day of 1842, John cut his finger shaving, and eleven days later died of lockjaw. Henry's care for his brother was extremely tender and his grief so deep that he contracted a sympathetic case of lockjaw eleven days following John's death, but he recovered.

After John died, Ralph Waldo Emerson, with whom Thoreau had first become friends in the fall of 1837, became his most important friend, and his great teacher. Thoreau lived for several periods as a handyman in Emerson's house and became a favorite of Emerson's children. Toward the end of his life, Emerson considered Thoreau to have been his best friend. Hawthorne lived nearby also, but he was never quite so fond of Thoreau. Emerson had bought a plot of ground on Walden shore, and Thoreau began building a cabin there in the early spring of 1845. He eventually moved in on July 4, 1845, and remained there, visiting Concord often, until September 6, 1847.

Leon Edel accuses Thoreau of concealing information about the number of his visits to the Thoreau family house and to Concord, implying that he was almost never alone, but no country person can read the winter sections without realizing that Thoreau experienced long times of winter solitude. Before and after his stay at Walden, he rambled incessantly through the Concord countryside, and eventually knew it so well that he took up part-time work as a surveyor, earning some money that way. Meanwhile he wrote in his journal, recording with intense dedication his observations during his long walks and setting down his thoughts. Writing two or three hours a day he completed fourteen volumes in printed form; it alone is an immense labor. In 1838 he gave his first lecture to the Concord Lyceum and in 1842 published his first major essay, "Natural History of Massachusetts," in the *Dial*. As a memorial to his brother, he turned his notes on their earlier river trip into the book called *A Week on the Concord and Merrimack Rivers*, and it became his first published book in 1849. In the same year his essay "Civil Disobedience" also appeared in print.

In practical life, Thoreau was amazingly able; he could construct, repair and invent with equal skill. When competition to the Thoreau pencil factory developed, he several times entered the business decisively, making improvements. Pencil makers had always split the cedar pencil-wood, put the lead paste into the grooves, and then glued the parts back together. Thoreau discovered a mixture of graphite and Bavarian clay that could be baked; then he invented a machine for drilling holes in the solid pencils into which he could insert the firmly baked graphite, saving the trouble of splitting and reglueing. He also developed pencils of varying hardnesses by increasing or decreasing the amount of clay. Thoreau pencils were considered the equal of English pencils, and Boston art teachers, it is said, required their students to buy only Thoreau pencils. The Thoreau firm received the Silver Medal for the best lead pencils at the Salem Charitable Mechanic Association of 1849, and all of this came about through Henry's practical genius, inventiveness and active interest in the firm.

After he moved out of his Walden cabin in September of 1847, Thoreau continued to work on *Walden*, and that book was published at last in 1854. When his father died in 1859, Thoreau immediately assumed the position of head of the family and manager of the family graphite business. He soon began to use stone rather than iron balls for grinding graphite, and so improved the lead once more. He also made some income by his lectures, traveling around New England on request. In 1859 he began defending John Brown in his lectures. In October of that year he announced a lecture on John Brown at the Concord Town Hall. When the Republican Town Committee and the Abolitionists both advised against it, he replied to them, "I did not send to you for advice, but to announce that I am to speak." When the selectmen refused to ring the bell, he rang it himself. On November 28 he arranged services at Town Hall on the day John Brown was to be executed in the South. Observing John Brown's moral honesty and the State's reaction to it led him to write even more vividly on the importance of resisting the State. His moral personality now became highly developed.

What can we say about his undeveloped side? We could say that even at the end of his life he had not come to any solid peace with his own body. In "Higher Laws" he wrote:

We are conscious of an animal in us, which awakens in proportion as our higher nature slumbers. It is reptile and sensual, and perhaps cannot be wholly expelled; like the worms which, even in life and health, occupy our bodies. Possibly we may withdraw from it, but never change its nature. I fear that it may enjoy a certain health of its own; that we may be well, yet not pure. The other day I picked up the lower jaw of a hog, with white and sound teeth and tusks, which suggested that there was an animal health and vigor distinct from the spiritual. This creature succeeded in other means than temperance and purity. "That in which men differ from brute beasts," says Mencius, "is a thing very inconsiderable; the common herd lose it very soon; superior men preserve it carefully."

A little farther on in this passage he attacks sexuality in a way implied by the earlier metaphors:

The generative energy, which, when we are loose, dissipates and makes us unclean, when we are continent invigorates and inspires us. Chastity is the flowering of man; and what are called Genius, Heroism, Holiness, and the like, are but various fruits which succeed it. Man flows at once to God when the channel of purity is open. By turns our purity inspires and our impurity casts us down. He is blessed who is assured that the animal is dying out in him day by day, and the divine being established.

It was as if he never took his body to be a part of nature. He would never have said, "Any woods is blessed that is assured that the animal in it is dying out day by day."

Yeats declared that every truth has its countertruth. We are given one truth, and the countertruth we have to develop; Yeats worked hard at developing his countertruth. The truth of the soul's interior abundance declared that we can have a love affair with the universe only if we decline to marry the world; that nature is the true friend of the soul; and the divine man is uncontrolled by social obligation. The countertruth might be: society is a deeper friend of the soul than nature; a man or a woman grows only if he or she is willing to give up a solitary affair with a shrub oak; no solitary self can replace society, social sensibility, manners and the institutions of Church and State. Had Thoreau lived longer, he might have developed that countertruth.

We could say also that Thoreau's soul, despite his immersion in nature, began to feel the lack of some moistness. Odell Shepard, in his collection called *The Heart of Thoreau's Journals*, comments: "Thoreau fills hundreds of pages in his last journals with minute notations of things measured and counted, mostly written in the lifeless style of professional scientists against which he had so often railed." Thoreau himself complained of dryness. In February 18, 1852, he wrote of the snow crust over rivers and ponds: "I can with difficulty tell when I am over the river. There is a similar crust over my heart." His fierce will gave him the power to break away from mean living, and he succeeded at that effort magnificently; but it was difficult for him to take in warmth from other men or from other women besides his mother and sisters, and one feels his soul, while remaining disciplined, grew increasingly isolated and thirsty. His love energy held on to nature, as he himself suggested by calling nature his bride.

But every writer has an undeveloped side. Emerson reported that a young Concord woman mentioned that taking Henry's arm was a little like taking the arm of an elm tree. She chose a slowly growing, tall and long-branched tree, a native American tree, as the image for him.

In February of 1860, Thoreau gave his newly completed "Wild Apples" lecture to the Concord Lyceum, and it turned out to be his last lecture there. On a lecture trip to Connecticut in September of 1860, he developed a cold and bronchitis, which activated his latent tuberculosis, and for the first time he could not take his long winter walks that year. A trip to Minnesota only made his tuberculosis worse, and when he returned in July of 1861 he was seriously ill. When Bronson Alcott visited him on New Year's Day of 1862, bringing cider and apples, he found Thoreau in bed and feeble, but talkative. They discussed Pliny and other rural authors. As long as Thoreau could sit up, he took his chair at the family table, saying, "It would not be social to take my meals alone." He also continued working on his Maine woods paper. Thoreau's last sentence contained the audible words "moose" and "Indian," and he died quietly on the evening of May 6, 1862, at the age of forty-four.

The Writings of Henry David Thoreau. Boston and New York: Houghton Mifflin and Company, 1906.

Atkinson, Brooks, ed. *Walden and Other Writings of Henry David Thoreau*. New York: Random House (The Modern Library), 1937.

Bode, Carl, ed. *Collected Poems of Henry Thoreau*. Enlarged ed. Baltimore: The Johns Hopkins University Press, 1964.

Bode, Carl, ed. *The Portable Thoreau*. New York: The Viking Press, 1980.

Harding, Walter. *The Days of Henry Thoreau: A Biography*. New York: Dover Publications, 1982.

INDEX OF POEMS AND PROSE SELECTIONS

Poem titles are printed in italics, and first words of prose passages are printed in roman type.